WallStreetBets

WallStreetBets:

How Boomers Made the World's Biggest Casino for Millennials

By: Jaime Rogozinski.

For information contact: wallstreetbets@gmail.com

ISBN: 9798606685684

First Edition: January 2020

To my wonderful wife, Alejandra,
and my beloved sons, Julian and Leonardo.

Without your love and support, none of this would be possible or even worth it.

There is nothing new on Wall Street or in stock speculation. What has happened in the past will happen again, and again, and again. This is because human nature does not change, and it is human emotion, solidly build into human nature, that always gets in the way of human intelligence. Of this I am sure.

—Jesse Livermore

TABLE OF CONTENTS

AUTHOR'S NOTE

If you've ever wondered about the existence of powerful cabals that are ensconced beyond perception yet yield tremendous influence, look no further than an antiquated and secret Internet Relay Chatroom. That's where you'll find the true masterminds behind WallStreetBets. The guys who still hang out there have been there since the subreddit was created. They are responsible for creating the humorous culture, high-profile shenanigans, and occasional meetups. They created and fostered the foundation for WallStreetBets's community, and without them it would not exist as we know it today. A group of virtual strangers online came together because of a common interest and, without realizing it, created something that has impacted the lives of many.

In order to meet online, they simply open a web browser and type in an address to interact. But over the years, members of this group became close and, on more than one occasion, met in person. They made the trek from Africa, Asia, Australia, Europe, and America to join random meetups and personal events.

To my good friends—park, talon, phaser, bacon, o2, rm, the russian, boshi, leesin, TL, greb, and rawb—thank you for the endless hours of fun, enlightening, educational, and inspirational conversations.

I also want to thank all the moderators, past and present, of WallStreetBets. It's a big community that relies on your volunteering, occasional trolling, sifting through complaints, designing style sheets, and enforcing rules.

Special thanks to CSV and OIU; may your wit, knowledge, and creativity always shine.

* * *

This book is not technical in nature. Readers don't need prior knowledge of finance or any of the concepts that are discussed in order to appreciate the message. The concepts used in this book are explained in simple terms along with easy-to-understand analogies as well as subtle humor. Although if you are completely new to finance, I'll warn that Chapter 7 is perhaps the trickiest one—so don't get discouraged by trying to understand every detail, it will all make sense at the end.

Lastly, some usernames and screenshots[1] used in this book have been changed to protect their identity. It is not my intention to ridicule people who have done outlandish things or lost large sums of money, nor is it to glorify those who walked away with huge wins. I use their stories to add entertaining real-life examples of many of the concepts described in the book, which at times can be somewhat complex. Both large losses and wins can have profound effects on people's lives, and for better or for worse, I don't take them lightly.

---

[1] Some screenshots have also been redacted for purposes of formatting.

1. A New Generation

> **MarketWatch** @MarketWatch
>
> On Reddit, he's "World Chaos," a high-schooler who turned $900 into $55K in just 12 days on.mktw.net/1VU30eM
>
> 3:15 AM - 5 Apr 2016

A New Generation

WORLD CHAOS

Four years ago, a high school student named Jeffrey made headlines after he publicly documented a lucky streak of wins online. On January 7, 2016, he made a post on social media's Reddit WallStreetBets forum titled "So I had 900 left in one of my accounts and decided to YOLO it." The acronym YOLO, which stands for You Only Live Once, is a popular term used in the forum. It is associated with making very risky trades, often resulting in an all-or-nothing outcome. In this case, the high-risk trade he made worked out in his favor, and he made an almost $3,200 profit overnight, leaving him with $4,000 in his account.

The following day he made a new post titled "I decided to YOLO again with the 4k from yesterday," which linked to a screenshot taken from his phone that showed he made roughly $5,500. His account value was now over $9,400.

Inside posts made on WallStreetBets, members of the forum actively participate in conversations by starting comment threads and replying to each other often using witty remarks. In a way, the rich interactions that take place in response to posts are what gives Reddit communities such strength.

The top comments in the post by world_chaos read:

Jeffrey, known as World_Chaos on WallStreetBets, accepted the challenge.

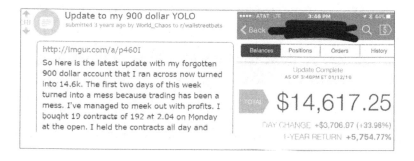

One day later, he made a new post titled "900 to 21k just in 10 days." Then the next day "Keep on yoloin' 900 to 30k." And finally, on his twelfth day, he made his final update with a final post "Y-O-FUCKING-LO, 900 to 55k in 12 days."

World_Chaos captured the hearts and minds of the WallStreetBets community and managed to encapsulate in six short posts what the community is all about. A high school kid had used the stock market and a lucky streak to take a few hundred dollars and turn it into $55,000 in less than two weeks.

A New Generation

WALLSTREETBETS

WallStreetBets has been called many things. Its known by the tagline "like 4chan found a Bloomberg terminal." This is a reference to an online forum linked to the notorious hacker group Anonymous having access to one of Wall Street's more sophisticated and exclusive trading platforms. Wall Street is the iconic symbol for the Financial District in New York and is generically used in finance when referring to topics related to the stock market. To those familiar with 4chan and Bloomberg, the slogan paints a picture of a mischievous gathering in total pandemonium with money being tossed around for careless or sometimes intentional reasons, all for the purpose of juvenile entertainment.

This picture is not entirely inaccurate. But it's also a superficial observation of a growing phenomenon with deeper roots that is becoming hard to ignore.

WallStreetBets (commonly referred to as WSB) is a large online forum or subreddit on Reddit; I started it back in early 2012 as an outlet for people to share high-risk investing or trading ideas. At the time, and to this day, most investing forums online take a conservative approach and tend to focus on the market as a long-term, diversified, wealth-growing ecosystem. What I was looking for was shorter term, a place where people could discuss the way to use the market in using more leverage and getting more action in less time. I was in my early thirties and single, and I had a decent disposable income and plenty of time on my hands.

Unbeknownst to me there was a big demand for this kind of community, and as a result WSB experienced impressive and entirely organic growth. As of November 2019, WSB had over 750,000 members, mostly millennials. Although traffic statistics suggest that the audience was much larger, with almost 2.9 million unique visitors in November 2019, this is probably due to third-party apps and using other methods that allow people to follow the subreddit without officially subscribing.

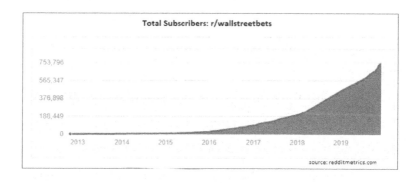

WSB is an eccentric community. It has grown into a quirky, meme-filled outlet where members share their massive monetary wins and losses (both are equally celebrated), trade ideas, arbitrage opportunities, and otherwise creative observations. It's common to see screenshots taken from users' cell phones, which they often use for trading, showing broker summaries and results of their massive trades (brokers are trading platforms that offer

A New Generation

people the ability to buy and sell stocks or other financial securities). Sometimes videos are uploaded to YouTube, where traders show their real-time reaction to massive losses (I've yet to see a reaction video of a huge win). They've also created their own lingo and often use crude, offensive language with complete disregard for people's political stances, religion, nationality, gender, sexual identity, mental disorders, etc. On this note, I'll take the opportunity to warn readers that many of the posts, comments, and screenshots included in this book are uncensored and include offensive language. Reader discretion is advised. Rest assured offensive language and insults chosen by the subreddit come and go in fads, cycling through all sorts of categories to offend without any rhyme or reason. In a way, you could say WSB members are unbiased, equal opportunity insulters.

Occasionally, WSB makes the news and is portrayed as a devious playground where children really shouldn't hang out. Here's a sample of headlines from the past few years:

- "Meet the Bros behind /r/WallStreetBets, Who Lose Hundreds of Thousands of Dollars in a Day—and Brag about It," [2] *Money Magazine*
- "You Probably Shouldn't Bet Your Savings on Reddit's 'Wallstreetbets' - Trading and trolling with the 4chan of finance," *Vice*

---

[2] On Reddit, community names are commonly referenced by their name and preceded by "r/"—as in r/wallstreetbets.

- "There's a Loud Corner of Reddit Where Millennials Look to Get Rich or Die Tryin'," *MarketWatch*
- "Reddit Thread Encourages Risky Millennial Traders to Make Insane Bets," *ValueWalk*

Matt Levine from Bloomberg wrote in an op-ed, "You should not underestimate the importance, in trading generally, of impressing people with your wit and boldness. For what do we live, but to make sport for r/wallstreetbets, and laugh at it in our turn?"

Around the same time, Josh Brown called members of WSB "psychopaths" during the program *Closing Bell* on CNBC.

So why does WSB have such a reputation? Probably because of the seemingly reckless behavior exhibited by the members, who proudly show off and encourage incredibly risky trades. Their behavior is also coupled with unfiltered attitudes about the market, which are shared with brutal honesty that I believe strikes a nerve with outside observers. The members also seem to have fun while engaging in this behavior, almost as if they were in a casino.

But I believe overall criticism of WallStreetBets is hypocritical, ageist, and classist. After all, the other guys are doing it too, on a much, much bigger scale.

A New Generation

Surprisingly got a call back from an investment bank
114
submitted 3 years ago to r/wallstreetbets

Second year MBA student, throwing my resume everywhere.
Bullet points at bottom of resume:

- Don't have 5 years experience in IB, but I've learned a lot when I lost 20k in January being long options.
- /r/wallstreetbets moderator.

Got an interview on Tuesday.

For example, in 2019 Morgan Stanley fired a twenty-seven-year-old trader named Scott Eisner after he lost $140 million on foreign exchange (forex) trades. Back in 2012, a single trader by the name of Bruno Iksil, who worked with JP Morgan, lost a whopping $6 billion due to a botched "hedging" strategy. In 2010 a futures trader named Stephen Perkins was banned and fined by the British Financial Services Authority for buying seven million barrels of crude oil, such a high volume that he pushed up the price of the commodity, during a drunken binge.

Have any of you guys ever tried trading while you're sober? I was thinking I might do better if I tried it.
1/0
submitted 3 years ago by PhalliusMaximus to r/wallstreetbets

What the youngsters on WSB do from their cell phones pales in comparison to what they could do if they were actually equipped with a fully loaded Bloomberg terminal as is the case with the so-called professionals.

There is nothing new about a select group of millennials (or anyone else for that matter) looking to have fun while gambling on Wall Street. Nonprofessionals simply never had the same opportunity to do so before. And now they are doing it publicly.

Wealth planner Alex Caswell of RHS Financial was quoted in a *Forbes* article in December 2019 saying "Robinhood and M1 Finance have built up cult-like followings among popular social media websites like Reddit. Some of these forums such as r/wallstreetbets take on a gambling-like theme where these reckless behaviors are born from."

Caswell is wrong—the reckless, gamblinglike behavior has always existed. It's just easier now, and WallStreetBets simply gives these people a place to hang out. And it provides visibility into a controversial topic with such brutal honesty that it makes people so uncomfortable that it becomes easier to label it as black sheep than to face more difficult questions.

What is driving this behavior? What are the incentives motivating the various participants involved? Is this a bad thing? Are there unknown systemic risks at play? Where are we heading toward? What can be done about it?

What appears to be a new phenomenon—that millennials are treating Wall Street like a casino—is really the confluence of three major factors: cultural attitudes toward Wall Street, easy access to the market through free brokers, and the proliferation of easy-to-use financial instruments.

A New Generation

2. Mindset

In the summer of 2010, WallStreetBets user TossOut5451 opened two trades for a total of around $170,000. He had a hunch about the economy reaching a turning point and decided to "go all in."

Around that time, the wounds from the financial crisis were still fresh for pretty much anyone with exposure to the financial system. Anyone with a pension fund or a mortgage, and anyone recently unemployed or recently graduated was in some way feeling the proverbial hangover from what can be described as a financial free-for-all party hosted by big banks playing with shiny instruments with fancy names.

Much has been said and written in the aftermath the 2008

crisis with lots of blame to go around. Common terms used during the finger-pointing exercises include Mortgage Backed Securities (MBS), Credit Default Swaps (CDS), Collateralized Debt Obligations (CDO), over leveraging, bank undercapitalization, subprime lending, blah blah blaheratization (BBB). Big words with little meaning to those who lost their jobs or homes. Some would argue those words had little meaning to those in the financial industry as well—perhaps they could define the terms if they were asked, but that's pretty much it.

The financial industry has been called irresponsible, akin to sixteen-year-olds with keys to fancy sports cars, which only they could drive. And it was these proverbial exclusive sports cars they were driving that had caused all the problems. It hadn't been some fad-driven craze like the dot-com bubble or the tulip mania experienced in the Dutch Republic during the 1600s or a crisis caused by some oppressive government like that of Venezuela today. It was only the banks and financial institutions that could play with and benefit from those instruments with fancy acronyms. It's what gave birth to the whole Occupy Wall Street movement. The movement represented a revolt against the few that had access to play with things that the masses did not. Some argue the anger around the movement revolved around the fact that society had to collectively pay for the irresponsible actions of the banks. That taxpayer bailouts were necessary to prevent complete global collapse. Wall Street was also the sole driver behind the wheel.

Mindset

In a 2010 New York Times op-ed titled "Gambling with the Economy," Roger Lowenstein compared the utility of Wall Street to that of a casino:

Wall Street's purpose, you will recall, is to raise money for industry: to finance steel mills and technology companies and, yes, even mortgages. But the collateralized debt obligations involved in the Goldman trades, like billions of dollars of similar trades sponsored by most every Wall Street firm, raised nothing for nobody. In essence, they were simply a side bet—like those in a casino—that allowed speculators to increase society's mortgage wager without financing a single house.

This sentiment has been echoed repeatedly in different ways throughout the years by different pundits, analysts.

Major motion pictures like *The Big Short* or *The Wolf of Wall Street* satirically protagonize the actions taken by industry insiders who use obscure financial system for personal gain and nothing more. These movies paint the industry insiders as being part of an exclusive casino to which most of society is not invited. Occupy Wall Street would agree.

It was also during this period when millennials were going to college, racking up student debt, forming opinions of the world, and shaping attitudes about Wall Street. It's entirely conceivable that this generation, or at least a large part of it, takes the financial system less seriously or has less respect for it than previous generations.

There's also something to be said about the financial profile of the average millennial. This generation has 8 percent less home ownership than its predecessor. It has $1.5 trillion in student debt, and its net worth is, on average, low.

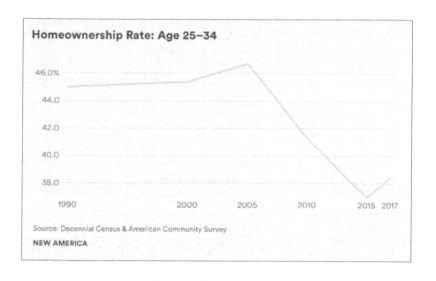

Homeownership Rate: Age 25–34

Source: Decennial Census & American Community Survey
NEW AMERICA

Even if a millennial had the best intentions of taking the stock market seriously with intentions of growing a worthy nest egg, the numbers are extremely discouraging. If we take the highest average net worth millennials—the thirty-eight-year-olds—and put their entire savings into stocks, they'd have to wait until they're nearly eighty to reach a half million dollars (assuming 10 percent annualized compound growth) before adjusting for taxes and inflation. If we assume the Fed continues its "NotQE"

Mindset

money-printing stimulus program forever, that retirement hardly seems appetizing.

Age	Average Net Worth
38 (Class of 2003)	$33,173
37 (Class of 2004)	$25,152
36 (Class of 2005)	$20,612
35 (Class of 2006)	$16,132
34 (Class of 2007)	$11,494
33 (Class of 2008)	$6,690
32 (Class of 2009)	$4,159
31 (Class of 2010)	$2,093
30 (Class of 2011)	-$1,989
29 (Class of 2012)	-$6,043
28 (Class of 2013)	-$10,168
27 (Class of 2014)	-$14,447
26 (Class of 2015)	-$18,988
25 (Class of 2016)	-$23,704
24 (Class of 2017)	-$28,706
23 (Class of 2018)	-$33,984
22 (Class of 2019)	-$38,915

On the other hand, a person of the same age with $1 million to invest today could retire quite comfortably with the $17 million he'd accrue with the same returns in thirty years.

If millennials aren't distrusting, they're at the very least disillusioned with the stock market.

In fact, Wells Fargo published a study in 2019 that found that 20 percent of young people, between ages twenty and thirty-six, said they will "never" be invested in the markets, 53 percent said they will "never be comfortable investing in the markets," and 70 percent said the Great Recession made them skeptical of stock-market experts.

This is the only good subreddit for finance that isn't filled with dogshit (self.wallstreetbets)
submitted 3 months ago by CarlCarbonite to r/wallstreetbets

302

I mean seriously have you guys checked r/personalfinance or r/stocks ? Both utter trash today. Boomers recommending 1.5% return crap to young people who would benefit from buying S&P 500 SPY ETF at its peak before a recession long term. 1.5%? Great so maybe I'll be able to double my money in like 50 years. Yay me. Nonsense buy fucking real stocks or SPY. Their recommendations are dog shit. We here offer the best thoughts, bigly thoughts. How can a bunch of a*****s know more about investing than "investing pros" on other subs. Even a high yield savings account is better than that shit.

TossOut5451 is no exception to this. In December 2019, he finally closed out his two trades and cashed out over $1.7 million.

He then explained "Still, I consider myself very lucky to have not lost everything. I would not make the same trade today seeing as how I am nearly 40 with significantly different priorities and risk appetite." A reasonable statement if his trades were indeed risky.

Here's what he actually did:

His first trade was to invest $100,000 into a fancy instrument (covered later) which, at the click of a single button, diversified his money into five hundred different stocks across eleven sectors and twenty-four industry groups. Then it magically magnified those returns threefold. It also pays dividends.

His second trade was to invest about $70,000 into a similar fancy instrument, which, at the click of a single button, diversified his money into large-cap financial companies and

Mindset

magically magnified those returns threefold as well.

So here you have a millennial who correctly takes an educated guess as to the timing of the economic recovery, as well as the recovery of financial industry. Then finds a couple of instruments to invest in that would, and did, literally make him lots of money if the condition "the economy improves" were true.

He then proceeds to very patiently make $1.7 million over a decade.

He then says he got lucky and would not do it again due to having lost his risk appetite.

TossOut5451 is in his own way a very wise and responsible individual, but his symbolic attitudes toward Wall Street and the stock market encapsulate that of his entire generation. He saw his successful, diversified, long-term investment as a YOLO gamble that he would not be willing to repeat given his life's changed circumstances. To be fair to TossOut5451, the instruments he chose that gave him the so called *magical magnified* returns did add an important risk component, which shouldn't minimized and will be covered later. In the coming chapters, you will learn about others with the same attitudes but entirely different levels of personal-risk tolerance.

Security	Quantity	Price	Price change	Value	Day's value change
SPXL DIREXION DAIL...	14,760	$66.93	$0.15 +0.23%	$987,888.28	$2,215.48 +0.23%
FAS DIREXION SHS...	7,464	$94.98	$0.20 +0.21%	$708,930.72	$1,492.80 +0.21%

Above is a screenshot TossOut5451 provided from his cell phone and uploaded to WallStreetBets to show the breakdown of his portfolio. The interesting thing about TossOut5451 and millennials in general is their willingness to share and engage such intimate details of their lives on social media.

UNCLE SAM

Millennials are not alone online though. The US government also does its part and tries to instill confidence in people through various means like using social media or passing laws. In efforts to stay away from highly polarizing political subjects, I won't pass judgment on the productivity of public Twitter bouts between the president of the United States and the chairman of the Federal Reserve regarding serious monetary policy although I'll point out these bouts do make for entertaining material on WSB.

Mindset

SEC Investor Ed @SEC_Investor_Ed

Don't understand an investment? Don't invest in it.

1:05 PM · Dec 10, 2019 · Hootsuite Inc.

Bloomberg

ETFs That Hide Their Portfolios Get Go-Ahead From U.S. Regulator

By Rachel Evans
December 10, 2019, 2:18 PM CST

If you asked the US government, it would probably say that gambling is bad.

Until recently, casinos were found in physically hard-to-define areas (like riverboats), Indian reservations, or a few select cities like Las Vegas or Atlantic City.

There have also been constantly evolving battles and shifting definitions in the space of online gambling. For decades, the United States relied on the Federal Wire Act of 1966, which courts have used to interpret various forms of online gambling as wire fraud.

In the early 2000s, with the combined growth in popularity of poker and widespread access to broadband internet, there was an ephemeral spike in online poker. During this time, Americans could gamble legally, but it did not take long before the government put a stop to it.

By 2006 the Bush administration passed the Unlawful Internet Gambling Enforcement Act (UIGEA) of 2006. The UIGEA says "unlawful internet gambling" means to place, receive, or otherwise knowingly transmit a bet or wager by means of the internet. The government's scorn toward online gambling under the Obama administration went as far as staging a theatric international crackdown in 2011 on online poker sites. In staging this crackdown, which required help from Interpol, the Obama administration seized $3 billion in assets and sought jail time for the site founders.

States that currently have laws explicitly prohibiting online gambling include Illinois, Indiana, Louisiana, Montana, Nevada (that's right), Oregon, South Dakota, Washington, and Wisconsin.

The pro-gambling lobby has had some victories, though. In May 2018, the Supreme Court overturned a law that prohibited sports betting in all states but Nevada.[3]

---

[3] Although this is still a gray area, individual states can legalize sports betting, but they are still in violation of the Wire Act,

Mindset

This all means that if adults in the United States feel the need to gamble, their choices are limited: they have to travel to a distant physical casino, figure out how to navigate and circumvent online gambling laws, or somehow get a job at a financial institution.

Or they could just open a brokerage account.

[−] **ThotianaPolice** [S] 48 points 7 hours ago

It doesn't change the fact that online gambling on slots and casino games is (practically) illegal in the US but, those same games are easier to understand than financial derivatives that these brokers are giving people access to that don't understand what they are buying.

   [−] **ixikei** 23 points 4 hours ago

   THIS! It blows me mind. Also makes me wonder why no one is selling financial derivative products OTC at convenience stores. These products could be packaged and sold and played very similar to current gambling products.

   Why does no one do this?

While the US government has gone to great lengths to regulate and deter any form of online gambling activities, it has turned a blind eye to what is arguably the world's largest casino: Wall Street. A great legal alternative where people can get their fix for free and online. Open twenty-four hours a day about six days a week, in all fifty states. The only requirements are being eighteen years old, having legal status in the United States, and having some money to spend.

Actually the US government not only turns a blind eye to these types of activities but also is, in fact, complicit in them. So why would the government care so much about a little wager on

---

which is a federal law for the operator. This is like challenges being faced by marijuana laws.

the Seattle Seahawks and not care if people are using Nasdaq like it's a slot machine? One word. Taxes.

The government could put a stop to this behavior, but instead it sets up the most lucrative tax system imaginable to benefit from Wall Street gamblers in ways that only those involved would understand. Even those involved in trading often learn about these tax rules once they get the bill from Uncle Sam for the first time.

It comes down to two components.

The first is the short-term capital gains tax rate being a lucrative 37 percent by the government. This is the rate traders face since they hold the securities for very short periods of time (sometimes minutes). This compares with the long-term capital gains rate used by regular investors, which, depending on various factors, can be as low as 0 percent.[4]

The second, and much more important component, is the little-known *wash-sale rule*. Essentially this rule says that traders cannot write off certain losses against certain trades if they were done within a thirty-day period of each other. More specifically if a trader exclusively trades Tesla shares every day, he would have to add up all the trades that turned a profit at the end of the year and pay 37 percent without being able to deduct the trades that lost money. This means traders can (and do) break even or lose money and still must pay a huge tax bill.

---

[4] Don't ask me how. Ask your accountant.

Mindset

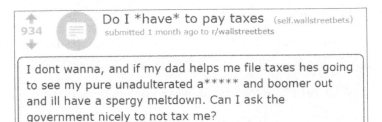

Do I *have* to pay taxes (self.wallstreetbets)

submitted 1 month ago to r/wallstreetbets

I dont wanna, and if my dad helps me file taxes hes going to see my pure unadulterated a***** and boomer out and ill have a spergy meltdown. Can I ask the government nicely to not tax me?

While this is a generalized explanation, there is some room for maneuvering around these components but not very much. One notable exception is when individuals qualify as traders with the Internal Revenue Service (IRS). Which on WallStreetBets is practically nobody.

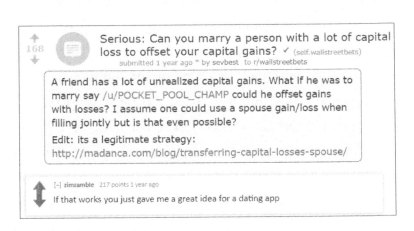

Serious: Can you marry a person with a lot of capital loss to offset your capital gains? ✓ (self.wallstreetbets)

submitted 1 year ago * by sevbest to r/wallstreetbets

A friend has a lot of unrealized capital gains. What if he was to marry say /u/POCKET_POOL_CHAMP could he offset gains with losses? I assume one could use a spouse gain/loss when filling jointly but is that even possible?

Edit: its a legitimate strategy:
http://madanca.com/blog/transferring-capital-losses-spouse/

[-] zimzamble 217 points 1 year ago
If that works you just gave me a great idea for a dating app

3. Access

In previous generations, a person looking to participate in the stock market would need a stockbroker, who would assess his financial goals, determine his investment-time horizon, and complete a slew of other time-consuming steps. Following up on a hunch for a stock would mean picking up the phone to ask a stockbroker to place an order to buy some shares and then paying a hefty commission for it to be executed.

Over the past decade, this has drastically changed. Fintech start-ups have forced their way into Wall Street and caused major disruptions, forcing major institutions to change the way they do business and offer easier access to their services at a lower or zero cost.

COMMISSION-FREE
TRADING

Robinhood is a revolutionary fintech start-up, which came to the market in late 2014 and was the first app-based broker to offer zero-commission trading for stocks in the United States and has since begun expanding the range of products it is offering. The founders of Robinhood were themselves affected by the 2008 financial crisis. It inspired them to enable people who were frustrated by the way the stock trading system was set up.

Rooted in this customer focus, we pioneered commission-free stock and ETF trading with no account minimums. And since then, we've added commission-free options trading, commission-free crypto trading through Robinhood Crypto.

It is an understatement to say it has had profound effects on the financial services industry. Major brokers, including E*Trade, TD Ameritrade, Charles Schwab, Fidelity, and more, have had to follow in Robinhood's footsteps and have begun to offer commission-free trading. There have also been similar start-ups, such as M1 Finance and Webull, which have used similar models.

There are a few interesting features that make Robinhood stand out. First, it is an entirely app-based broker, which largely targets millennials. That is, users cannot download computer software or place phone calls to make trades—all trading is done exclusively on cell phones (or web browsers). Second, Robinhood has no readily available phone support. For help, users can send messages via the app, email, or social media. Users can open an account with no minimum deposit, and the process for funding an account is relatively easy and provides users with instant access to trading.

Robinhood has had tremendous success. It has surpassed all other US brokers (in number of accounts), reaching 10 million users in 2019. Nearly double what it had in 2018. Their growth

Access

rate is nothing short of impressive, but there is something worth noting: the growth of WallStreetBets.

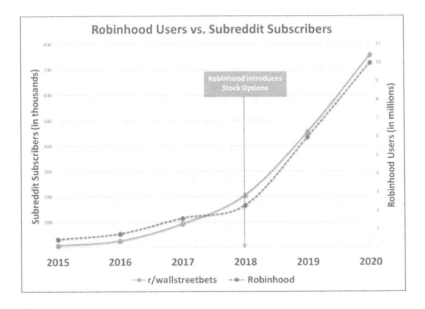

While it's important not to conflate causation and correlation, it's also hard to ignore the nearly identical adoption rate on Robinhood and subscriber growth rate on WallStreetBets. This includes the spike and coinciding slope after Robinhood introduced stock options in 2018.

Keep in mind that Robinhood is not the only zero-commission broker. Zero-commission trades are now the standard offering of virtually all US brokers for trading stocks, and many are following with stock options.

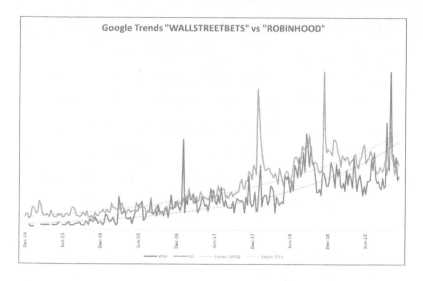

Thanks to Robinhood, there's a competitive race going on between brokers, with rapid changes and new offerings coming at a fast pace. Currently stocks and options seem to be dominating the offering, but it probably won't be long before they move into futures, forex, bonds, or new creative types of securities.

PEEWEE LEAGUE

It's not just access to zero-commission brokers but also the barriers of entry that used to exist in the form of capital requirements. Twenty years ago, people needed a fair amount of money to dabble with the market. Trading stocks required maybe $60 in commissions round trip ($30 for buying and $30 selling), which meant anything less than $10,000 would make little sense.

Access

Otherwise trading with small amounts meant the cost of commissions would eat a huge percentage of the potential earnings. Futures traders needed account balances of at least $25,000 to be approved for the margin requirements and to be able to withstand the whipsaw associated with the highly leveraged instruments. Protective stock options on expensive shares (like Amazon which is currently trading just below $2,000 per share) can cost thousands of dollars per contract. In other words, it was a big boys' club.

Having the sums of money necessary to participate in these activities comes with certain assumptions. A person who deposits $25,000 into his account likely has a certain age and education level, statistically speaking. He may also have an established personal-risk tolerance. Perhaps someone who has $25,000 saved up in the first place has some semblance of fiscal responsibility.

Big boys can afford fancy toys as well, like their own cars and nice laptops or the latest OctaCam cell phones. But there was a time when those big boys weren't big and couldn't afford those toys or fancy brokerage accounts.

Clara Bullrich of Alvarium Investments was quoted in a 2019 *Forbes* article saying, "Commission-free investing apps come with more advantages that may not be obvious. For example, they give you the opportunity to invest in the markets regardless of the size of your bank account."

Companies can be quite aggressive and creative when

marketing to children at a young age. Brands and products try to hook kids when they're young and not worried about money, so when they're older and able to make their own decisions, they're already loyal. College students get attractive discounts for Microsoft Office products and Apple laptops because, once they're in an ecosystem, it's difficult to turn back.

In the brokerage world, there is a silent movement growing that appears to be taking a page out of that same peewee-league playbook. After all, how can kids play with the market if they can't afford it?

Are you broke but still interested in playing with index futures? Are you bummed out because you can't afford the minimum buy-in rate to play? Look no further; the Chicago Mercantile Exchange just launched the aptly named E-Micro futures available May 2019.

If someone is interested in gambling on Wall Street, here are the current market offerings. No commissions on stocks. No commissions on options. No account minimums. Fractional share purchases (for those expensive stocks). Mini options contracts. Mini futures contracts. Micro futures contracts. Mini forex lots. Micro forex lots.

To give you an idea what this means using index futures, the original S&P futures contract, commonly used by large institutions, exposes traders to $250 for every $1 move in the index. That is, if the index goes from $3,000 to $3,001, then the owner of an S&P contract will make $250. A "mini" lot, which

Access

is the most commonly used, exposes traders to $50 to $1 leverage. And finally, the new micro lots give traders a mere $5 for every $1 move in the index.

Some of these products aren't new, but some are very new.

You may have taken issue with my choice of words. After all, there are legitimate reasons for having zero commissions as well as fractional share purchasing. And it's true. For example, Acorn is a service that also offers fractional share purchasing is a noble cause meant to be a nest egg to promote savings. Fractional share purchasing is a relatively novel concept that allows people to buy fractions of a share, which is useful when people can't afford complete ones.[5] You'll be hard-pressed to find their margin requirements listed in Acorn's Terms of Service.

There is no legitimate reason for any broker or financial institution to offer E-Micro futures or mini options contracts for any reason other than to make gambling more affordable and accessible to the masses. Simply put, fiscal responsibility is no longer a prerequisite for those looking to YOLO using complex and highly risky financial securities.

Making a lower threshold to trade also widens the range of eligible customers for brokers. And indeed, brokers have cast a wider net to capture customers. Recently, there was an ad for Robinhood spotted on the latest teen-sensation app TikTok,

---

[5] The most obvious example would be Warren Buffett's Berkshire Hathaway—a single share is currently valued at over $340,000.

whose latest demographics show 60 percent of users being between the ages of sixteen and twenty-four.

Tara Falcone, a certified financial planner and founder of ReisUP, said of Robinhood, "I liken it to giving the keys of a sports car to a 12-year-old." That's bit of an exaggeration. In all the research for this book, I did not find a single twelve-year-old who has played with the stock market using real money.

But I did find a thirteen-year-old.

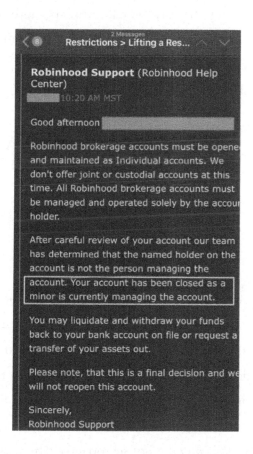

Access

Above is a screenshot a thirteen-year-old sent me from an email message he received from Robinhood, after his account was canceled shortly after a certain incident. Out of consideration to him, I'm choosing not to disclose further details of the story. Even if I attempted to conceal his username, it would be easy for people to piece together who he is, given that this incident was very high profile and received attention from the media.

It suffices to say that the overall efforts by both brokers and providers of financial instruments to create wide-ranging and affordable access to the markets have proven to be and continue to be tremendously successful.

ACCOUNT APPROVAL

 Td ameritrade made me apply to enable options. I told them I have no experience, make less than $20k per year, and have 5 dependents. They approved options trading immediately. (self.wallstreetbets)
submitted 1 year ago by alandi

While I decided to omit the high-profile story of the teenage Robinhood trader, the same question repeatedly came up: how is it possible that people like this get approved for these sorts of high-risk trades involving stock options? Options are extremely complicated instruments that, depending on how they're used, can range from being safe Warren-Buffet-investment-grade instruments to "playing the house" on a roulette table and being on the hook for paying other players' potential winnings.

The Financial Industry Regulatory Authority (FINRA) attempts to address this specific point with Rule 2090: Know Your Customer.

> Every member shall use reasonable diligence, in regard to the opening and maintenance of every account, to know (and retain) the essential facts concerning every customer and concerning the authority of each person acting on behalf of such customer.

The purpose of this rule is to protect both the customers as well as the brokers. While it's debatable how much FINRA truly intends to protect unwitting traders from blowing their accounts, it does have good reason to protect the brokers from exposure to reckless traders. After all, stock options are a class of financial derivatives that have underlying risks and fancy acronyms. Stock options are digital contracts signed by parties and counterparts; they have conditions and obligations to be met. People place bets with options, and they expect to be paid if they win. Failure to meet these obligations would fracture confidence in the entire financial system, like what arguably happened in 2008 with American International Group (AIG), when the sole "financial insurance provider" was in no condition to pay out the barrage of incoming claims being filed. In other words, for the system to work, people need to trust that deals and agreements will be kept.

Access

The system is at risk if insolvent kids are allowed to make promises to buy or sell millions of dollars' worth of stocks that they aren't able to deliver. A casino is likely to collapse the moment the roulette dealer fails to pay out winners due to insufficient collateral at the time he or she was taking people's bets.

So FINRA makes the brokers know their customers, and subsequently brokers make their customers fill out a questionnaire before allowing them access to risky stuff. With stock options, account levels typically range from numbers one through four or five. The higher the number, the riskier it gets. The problem is that the rule is vague, and brokers have a lot of discretion when it comes to writing guidelines for it. Problems are compounded when factoring in the perverse incentives brokers have in the face of mounting competition to get younger generations of investors with herculean personal-risk tolerances. In other words, brokers need to protect themselves and their customers in order to make sure Wall Street continues to function while simultaneously attracting members of the riskiest trading demographic and giving them free reign to do as they please in order to lure them in. A moral hazard in the purest form.

The customers, on the other hand, face an easier ethical conundrum. They know full well the level of risk they want their account to be approved for, and they will stop at nothing until they get it. They're like patients looking for prescription painkillers who go from doctor to doctor, making up stories until they find the right combination.

Access

4. Leverage

The goal for most successful day traders and recreational gamblers alike is to find ways to make or lose money as quickly and easily as possible. Luckily for them, Wall Street offers no shortage of options to accomplish this (pun intended).

For example, professional traders, the ones who rely on trading for a living, tend to trade securities called *futures*[6] for several advantageous reasons. Futures are traded in high volume, which reduces the spread between the buy and sell price (it saves money), and increases the chance of the buy and sell price being matched up at the prices traders want. But the biggest attraction to trading futures is most likely the *leverage* they get, since arguably the two benefits mentioned can also be found by simply trading shares of popular stocks.

---

[6] The definition of futures is not important. The only important thing is that they trade like many other things in the market. They have prices, and they move up and down like everything else, which gives people a chance to speculate.

Leverage can be roughly translated to risk/return. In other words, it's a way to calibrate the speed at which traders can make or lose their money.

Let's suppose a person wanted to rely solely on trading income to make a living. To make $60,000 per year by trading stocks that offer no leverage (or one-to-one leverage), a person would need a difficult combination of factors. One such combination would require her to have a $100,000 account and make 5 percent each month. This requires having a lot of capital and a very impressive trading record.

Alternatively, if she were to use leverage like the kind offered with futures (in the United States it is typically fifty-to-one), the goal would become much more realistic. The same annual income could be attained by making just 1 percent monthly on a $10,000 account. The catch, of course, is that she can lose her money just as fast (e.g. if she loses 1 percent in a month, she loses half her money).

Another advantage of leverage, especially in higher amounts, is the apparent speed at which a trade can move—which obviously magnifies the thrill. This is especially important to day traders since stocks and markets on average don't tend to move all that much during the day. And often when there are big moves, they take place overnight when the markets are closed.[7]

---

[7] Some securities can be traded when markets are closed, and others cannot.

Leverage

Trade Size	Leverage	Price Move	Profit/Loss
$1,000	1:1	1%	$10
$1,000	50:1	1%	$500
$1,000	100:1	1%	$1,000
$1,000	500:1	1%	$5,000

There are many other ways to get leverage at varying levels besides futures. This will be discussed in the coming chapters.

Thank you fellow gamblers for introducing me to day 0 options trading, 2.5k in 5 mins.. (i.redd.it)
submitted by golden_state7 to r/wallstreetbets

The question I've asked myself is why haven't more people on WallStreetBets taken a liking to using futures? They're very attractive for a wide variety of reasons, and they're heavily preferred among professionals. They come with all the advantages and few of the disadvantages of stock options, which are so popular on the subreddit.

The answer, I believe, is because they're not as accessible.

Not all brokers offer access to futures, and the ones that do place a higher burden, in the form of capital and experience, on the client to qualify them.

OPTIONS

On the topic of leverage, no instrument is more interesting and popular on WSB than stock options. They're widely available and included in the zero-commission trading on many platforms, and they can be used in complex strategies and can offer massive amounts of leverage. Hence, they're a favorite on the subreddit.

Although it can be helpful but for the purposes of this book, it's not necessary to understand how these things work. There is enough literature out there that covers this topic ad nauseam, so instead I'll use case-specific analogies to help decipher how they're used in various situations.

In their most basic form, stock options work like insurance. They offer an inexpensive solution to purchase nonrefundable coverage for people to protect their investments in case of catastrophic downturns. Due to their leverage structure, they're also used by speculators to make relatively cheap bets in hopes for profit. And unlike futures they're widely available to the masses, with minimal approval requirements to trade. For now,

Leverage

all you need to know is that there are two types of stock options: *call options* and *put options.* Call options are purchased by people who are betting on the prices of something going up. Otherwise known as being "bullish" on the street. Put options, on the other hand, are purchased by people who are betting on the prices of something going down. This sentiment is known as being "bearish."

Buying calls = betting on prices rising = bullish.

Buying puts = betting prices dropping = bearish.

That's all for now.

The reason options are attractive is because people can make all sorts of fun combinations. People can both buy and sell them; that is, they can place bets, or they can take bets that someone else places. They can simultaneously buy and sell puts and calls, with various parameters that produce the most bizarre results. Options can be used responsibly, and they can be used irresponsibly. Various combination strategies also come with cool names like spreads, butterflies, iron condors, straddles, and strangles, which sound like Brazilian Jiu-Jitsu moves.

WHAT IF *STAR WARS* BOMBS?

Plenty of the high-stakes risk takers on WSB know exactly what they're doing. In some cases, they've demonstrated a deeper understanding of the financial instruments than many professionals. This is certainly the case with all the people who try to game the system (more on this later). Then there're other cases where people are willfully ignorant about their actions and know full well that what they are doing is, in some way or another, risky without understanding why. And often they don't want to understand.

But occasionally there are stories where well-intentioned people, who try to do the right thing, end up in the WSB spotlight without it having been their intention. This was the case with Reddit user CrystalBaller.

CrystalBaller is not even a member of WallStreetBets; in fact he has never posted on the subreddit. Instead he hangs out with the older, more responsible, and much more boring brother of a forum—r/investing.

Reddit's Investing forum is the antithesis of WSB. The subreddit is focused on low-risk, long-term time horizon, dividend-paying, well-diversified, fixed-income talk that puts gamblers to sleep. It often finds itself the butt of WSB jokes and finds itself to be the bully scapegoat when people there try to bring up conversations that give off any hint of academia.

Here's the post CrystalBaller made:

Leverage

Bought Disney options, messed up badly (self.investing)

Bought 10 shares of Disney, then I buy 10 protective put options cause I figure I wanna reduce the risk of a bad Star Wars 9... Instead I buy 10 whole new shares of Disney along with it? And worse, immediately stuck with a $300 loss for overpaying for puts.

This is what we're looking at: https://imgur.com/4x6xtZP

Not the worst thing in the world, wanted to learn options and just went with it. But I goofed pretty badly. Now I just wanna know what to do with this... It's kinda just there.

Update, looking over it again I just bought a call. I think it's the opposite of a put but I'm not too sure on the specifics.

192 comments share save hide give award report crosspost

Don't bother trying to understand of what he wrote; it makes no sense.

Here's what he did. Our unintended hero purchased ten shares of Disney. A $260 billion company, which pays dividends and has a price-to-earnings ratio (P/E) of twenty-two. In other words, a very reasonable long-term investment, which cost him around $1,500. He then decided to "buy insurance" on his ten shares by buying ten *puts*. Instead he mistakenly bought ten *calls*.

To gain access to buy options, brokers often make their customers agree to some extra terms of service and click an extra "I Agree" during the installation of the app.[8]

Options are great for both insurance and for gambling because they're leveraged—with little money, users can control

---

[8] This varies, but for all intents and purposes, it's relatively easy to get approved.

a lot of shares. More specifically, each option's contract value is calculated using blocks of one hundred shares. CrystalBaller just purchased ten options contracts. Each contract controls one hundred shares of Disney for a grand total of one thousand shares (plus, of course, his ten original shares he was trying to protect).

This conservative investor who wanted to protect his $1,500 investment in a dividend-paying, large-cap company was now welding $150,000 worth of stock. And, as of the time he made the post, he still didn't realize it.

How is this possible? Because he didn't need $150,000 in his account. He only needed $3,150 to buy the ten call options. That's how options work. After realizing he had no idea what he was doing, he quickly sold everything off. When this was all finished, twenty-four minutes later, he was baffled to have made a $180 profit.

> [−] **CristalBaller** [S] 27 points
> So this just happened: https://imgur.com/c9FFYFE
> I'm absolutely stunned. I just fell ass backwards into a $200 profit and have no idea what even happened.
> Not sure how I only got 10, I entered just 10 instead of 100.
> permalink embed save parent report give award reply

This story had a happy ending, but the moral is tragic. A guy tried to protect his ten Disney shares in case the Star Wars movie sucked and ended up controlling $150,000 worth of shares

Leverage

instead. By accident. This is an investor who was trying to be responsible and was well intended.

ORDER STATUS	All Orders	⌄	(Drag to reorder)							
Action	Qty	Symbol	Description	Order	Bid	Ask	Dur.	Date	Status	Executed
SLD to Close	10	DIS Call	DIS Dec 27 2019 144.00 Call	Limit $3.30	3.05	3.20	Day	12/10/19 10:21 AM ET	Executed	$3.33
BOT to Open	10	DIS Call	DIS Dec 27 2019 144.00 Call	Market	3.05	3.20	Day	12/10/19 9:57 AM ET	Executed	$3.15

These sophisticated tools are made so accessible and tempting that they successfully lured an unwitting investor into making a dangerous and potentially catastrophic decision with his portfolio.

There's something else worth pointing out. CrystalBaller uploaded his post to r/investing looking for advice right after he made his mistake, while his trade was still open. He turned to the internet for help avoiding a loss of money. Even though his broker is the kind that provides free phone support, he found it more sensible to ask strangers for help. This speaks volumes about the collaborative trust instilled in peers with no credentials over formal *boomer* institutions. It gives additional insight into the thought process and mind-set of millennials.

CrystalBaller is not the only case of a youngster turning to the internet for help. Visit any forum on reddit, and you'll find tons of examples—and not just stock-related forums. People turn to cyber strangers for help with school, career, legal, tax, relationship, and other life-altering matters.

OOPS, I MADE SOME MONEY

A WSB hall-of-famer named flipper321 got the community's attention when he scored a solid $110,000 win by using options. What really made his case unique was that he had no idea how he did it. For an example on how trading stock options carry risks that beginners often don't understand, here's how things went down. On February 8, 2018, he wrote:

I somehow made $110k this morning and I'm still not totally sure how (self.wallstreetbets)
submitted 1 year ago to r/wallstreetbets
399 comments share save hide report

Yesterday at 4:10pm EST I sold the 266.50/266.00 put spread for a 2 cent credit. 1,000 of them. I guess at 4:14 or 4:15 before the option expired SPY must've dipped below 266.50 because I woke up the next morning before the market opened and saw my balance was up about $140k. I thought it was a glitch with the Etrade app at first but then looked at my portfolio and saw what happened. For some reason I was assigned only 863 of the 1000 put contracts I sold. That's 86,300 shares of SPY which is about $23,000,000 worth. I only had $50,000 in my account so I started panicking and wondering if Etrade would liquidate my account or something, so I put in a limit order of 268 (SPY was trading around 268.12 at the time), hoping the sale

Leverage

would go through immediately. After putting in the order a message popped up saying my order would be put through when the market opened, which I don't understand because I thought you could buy and sell stocks/ETFs during premarket hours. So anyway I was stuck staring at my phone's screen until 9:30 when the market opened. Immediately about half my shares sold for $268 each. The market seemed to be dropping so I lowered my limit for the rest to 267.60 and the rest of them sold for that price. After all that my balance was about $112k higher than it was yesterday. Does anyone know how much interest Etrade will charge me for holding 23 million dollars of SPY for these few hours?

Then he attached a picture as proof:

Date	Type	Description (show categories)	Amount ($)
02/08/18	Sold	-43033 of SPY @ $267.60	11,515,354.71
02/08/18	Sold	-50 of SPY @ $268.0099	13,400.18
02/08/18	Sold	-200 of SPY @ $268.0107	53,600.88
02/08/18	Sold	-100 of SPY @ $268.0455	26,803.92
02/08/18	Sold	-21 of SPY @ $268.0599	5,629.12
02/08/18	Sold	-1500 of SPY @ $268.04	402,050.53
02/08/18	Sold	-50 of SPY @ $268.0657	13,402.97
02/08/18	Sold	-40946 of SPY @ $268.00	10,973,264.69
02/08/18	Sold	-400 of SPY @ $268.015	107,203.47
02/08/18	Assignment	863 PUT SPY 02/07/18 266.50 STANDARD & POORS DEPOSITOR...	0.00
02/08/18	Expiration	10 PUT SPXW 02/07/18 2530 CBOE S&P 500 CLOSE/EURO IND...	0.00
02/08/18	Expiration	137 PUT SPY 02/07/18 266.50 STANDARD & POORS DEPOSITOR...	0.00
02/08/18	Expiration	2 PUT SPXW 02/07/18 2680 CBOE S&P 500 CLOSE/EURO IND...	0.00
02/08/18	Expiration	10 PUT SPXW 02/07/18 2535 CBOE S&P 500 CLOSE/EURO IND...	0.00
02/08/18	Expiration	1000 PUT SPY 02/07/18 266 STANDARD & POORS DEPOSITORY O	0.00
02/08/18	Expiration	2 PUT SPXW 02/07/18 2675 CBOE S&P 500 CLOSE/EURO IND...	0.00
02/08/18	Bought	86300 of SPY @ $266.50	-22,998,954.95
02/07/18	Sold Short	1000 SPY Feb 07 '18 $266.50 Put(SPY) @ $0.05	4,478.71
02/07/18	Bought To Open	1000 SPY Feb 07 '18 $266 Put(SPY) @ $0.03	-3,519.17
02/07/18	Sold Short	1 SPXW Feb 07 '18 $2680 Put(SPX) @ $0.10	8.95

I'll interpret. First, the acronym SPY is the ticker symbol for a type of share that tracks the S&P 500, which is a collection of well-diversified stocks like the kind used by TossOut5451. In summary, he had $50,000 in his E*Trade broker account, and he made a large bet trying to pick up pennies in front of a steamroller without fully understanding what he was doing. More specifically, he made a bet that, in theory, had a maximum possible profit of about $1,000 and a maximum loss of about $49,000 (factoring in commissions which he paid). But he wasn't trading on a theoretical broker; he was trading in real life, where things work differently. On paper, he risked his entire account in hopes of increasing it by just 2 percent. The following day, he had $23 million worth of shares in his account because part of his bet was selling options (taking bets that other people placed). To meet his obligation, E*Trade had to loan flipper321 $23 million for several hours while he closed out his trade.

The comments in the thread were insightful:

"Lol, why would you sell a spread for .02 credit? Does that even cover your commissions at eTrade? Sounds like you lucked out hard, but regarding your question, you should ask eTrade," someone said.

Flipper321 replied, "I thought I was being safe. I just wanted to scalp a few pennies."

"That's like running into Chernobyl a few minutes before complete meltdown because you forgot your wallet."

Leverage

A few months later, flipper321 came in with a follow-up for those who were curious.

I was charged $9,823.21 in interest. It still seems like a lot for only holding SPY for a few hours, but I can't complain about $102k in profit. I'll pay the tax next year, but since I lost $85k last year (don't wanna get into that) I won't pay much tax. I never got a phone call from Etrade.

What he did was sell put options that expired the following day with the hopes that the price of SPY would not fall (don't be confused by this; it's like a double negative—*selling* put options as opposed to *buying* them means he's actually bullish). Just in case, he also bought slightly cheaper put options that expired the following day as insurance to cap his losses. Selling options, as opposed to buying them, is the equivalent of being the roulette dealer at a casino. Sellers of options are responsible for paying out the winners—potentially unlimited amounts of money. To protect against unlimited losses, flipper321 also *bought* some cheaper put options as well. The trader plays both the roulette dealer by selling options and roulette player by buying options. He takes advantage of the price differences in order to make a little money and hopes that none of the players win. But if a player does win, then he will also win (just not as much) and is responsible for paying the predefined difference.

Flipper321 tried this strategy one thousand times over, using a tool that gave him one hundred times leverage. Both he and his broker found out that what works on paper doesn't always translate to real life. The following morning, he found that 863 people had "won" the roulette game he was hosting, but he did not win a single one of his "insurance" bets. In order to pay the winners at the table, his broker had to lend him the $23 million. However, the trading day was still open, and his seemingly innocent bet was now an unsafe, messy spider web of open positions he didn't fully understand. By Friday morning he still owed and owned lots of put options that expired that day, and he had in his possession a whole lot of shares that never expire. He made money because of his quick thinking and was lucky the market did not move against him early in the day.

> ↑ [-] **flipper021** 62 points 1 year ago
> ↓ I wonder what would happen if I held SPY to the end of the day, since I'd be holding a paper loss of $800k, but I'm not willing to find out.

Ultimately, flipper321's broker lent him the money and let him decide how to close out the trade, at his sole discretion. Flipper321 could have easily lost hundreds of thousands of dollars if he had handled it differently or if the market had gone against him. Maybe E*Trade thinks its users know what they're doing. Either way, this type of trade is common, and how brokers choose to handle these scenarios is a matter decided by their internal policy and can vary widely. With these types of

Leverage

options trades, brokers are on the hook for this assignment risk, which is calculated based on theory and has a maximum profit and loss potential. This theory makes assumptions about certain market conditions as well as traders on both sides of the options trades acting rationally and/or knowledgeably.

[−] thunderwurst_noine 33 points 17 days ago
Tell fucking Etrade to stop making tv commercials with retards on yachts if they are not fully equipped to deal with retards trying to make yacht money.

F D

FDs should stand for Fire Departments because they burn. Instead, the acronym[9] refers to a certain sexual act associated with the expected outcome of trading this options strategy. The first reference to this type of trade appeared several years ago, when a member of WSB was trying to make an educational post outlining various way in which people can trade options. In the post, he explained the basics of options and then included a chart with several possible trade ideas.

---

[9] As to what it stands for, I'm leaving it to your imagination.

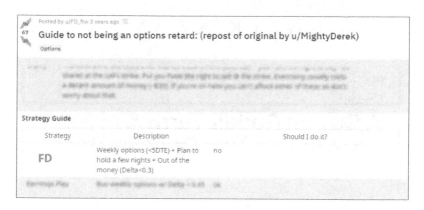

Strategy Guide

Strategy	Description	Should I do it?
FD	Weekly options (<5DTE) + Plan to hold a few nights + Out of the money (Delta<0.3)	no

As you can see, the author did two things to try to dissuade WSBers from this strategy. First, the distasteful name that he gave the options strategy. The second, a clear "no" in the column titled "Should I do it?"

Needless to say, this is now one of the most popular strategies used on WSB trade options. Rather than explain the mechanics of the strategy, I'll use another analogy.

Trading *FDs* is the equivalent of buying hurricane insurance that is valid for five days for houses in Colorado, in the middle of spring, with no hurricanes being forecasted. The idea is simple; the insurance is very cheap (and therefore losses are relatively capped), and if for some freak reason a hurricane appears out of nowhere, the insurance payouts can be massive. These are also often compared to buying scratch-off lottery tickets. They're highly leveraged, and when they win, which isn't often, they lead to massive payouts. This was the case with WSB user TheTriviaTribe.

Leverage

WALK AWAY

TheTriviaTribe is in his midtwenties, works as a professional in a field unrelated to the stock market, and became interested in trading a few years ago. He joined WSB and started teaching himself about stocks and options and eventually decided to throw some money at this game.

As is the case with most people who start (and most who continue), TheTriviaTribe lost money. He lost an amount that he could afford to lose, about $10,000 over the course of two years, which he chalked up to his tuition for a hands-on learning experience. Unlike others on WSB who develop an obsession with the market, his approach was humbler, almost as if he realized the money he was spending would likely never be recovered.

Some people who lose money in the market have similar emotional states to those of gamblers or poker players. Often going on *tilt*, which is a form of desperation after suffering big losses. This was not the case at all with TheTriviaTribe. It was the opposite.

On Thursday, September 19, he deposited $1,000 into his

broker account on a hunch that Roku's price would go down the following day. He lost a bit of money on some other trades that day before finally taking his remaining $766 and betting it all on *FDs*. In order to make money, the price of Roku had to have a very sharp fall the following day, or he would lose it all.

 [-] manojk92 142 points 3 months ago
Position?

 [-] TheTriviaTribe [S] 392 points 3 months ago
I got some $111, $114, $120, $124, $126, and $128 puts for really cheap yesterday expiring today. Lucky day, but I'm not going to complain.

You might remember the freak "bomb cyclone" that hit Denver with hurricane-force winds in the middle of spring in 2019. That's exactly what happened with Roku. The following day, it fell nearly 20 percent and TheTriviaTribe's $766 had made him close to $50,000.

A couple days later, he let his luck ride and made a large bet, albeit much safer (not *FDs*), that the S&P 500 would go down and indeed was right. The stocks had an intraday fall of nearly 2 percent, and using a similarly leveraged options play, he more than doubled his money.

This was very lucky and impressive, but what TheTriviaTribe did next was one of the most surprising things I've seen someone do on WSB.

For most people it is extremely difficult to contain the

Leverage

feelings of elation associated with making large sums of money in a short amount of time. Even for seasoned professionals, the overwhelming sensation and excitement can often turn into a state of carelessness and feelings of invulnerability, which lead to making foolish trades. At the very least, suddenly having access to a much larger account balance can also lead people to forget the value of money and act equally irresponsibly.

TheTriviaTribe was not impervious to this effect. He had trouble concentrating at work, started making reckless trades, and ended up losing about $15,000 in the process. But instead of making matters worse, he did the most sensible thing that a person could do. He withdrew his money, threw it into his retirement fund, and went back to work. TheTriviaTribe has not made any trades since his big win and said, "I decided I'm only going to invest in future savings I get."

In other words, what TheTriviaTribe did was to treat Wall Street as a casino in the most literal form. He learned about how to play a particular slot machine and lost some money in the process. Then he made a lucky bet and hit the jackpot. Twice. With that much capital in his retirement fund, compounded over several decades, the payoff can be quite significant. TheTriviaTribe knows he got lucky and will likely never be able to repeat the trade, nor did he allow delusions of grandeur to cloud his thoughts.

JUST ~~ONE~~ ~~TWO~~ THREE MORE

While it is entirely possible that the wisdom and maturity displayed by TheTriviaTribe to be able to walk away from winning two consecutive jackpots was congenital in nature, he may have had a helping hand in the form of watching other winners before him.

Rectalcropper2 is a self-described twenty-year-old student who months ago was seen in the r/tax subreddit asking about how to file taxes for last year's modest four-figure trade-related gains. At first glance his 2018 profits were respectable for a college student, but a deeper dive reveals the rocky, less enviable road he took to achieve them.

He made his debut on Reddit with his account one year ago when he made his first post, dated August 27, 2018, on WSB:

Leverage

Over the weeks he updated the subreddit with play-by-play trades he was making with varying success, along with his unfiltered mind-set at every point in time.

"Can people stop making money?" he pleaded at one point. "This sub isnt fun when we arent posting our rh accounts getting cucked" (RH being the abbreviation for Robinhood). About a month after his original post he asked, "Anyone else becoming numb to the pain?"

By the end of 2018, this is roughly what his trading history looked like:

Rectalcropper2's post linked to a screenshot from his phone, which showed the all-time history for his account balance along with a visual representation of it in the form of a graph. His journey begins with an estimated account balance of $24,000. The picture portrayed what appears to be a good start to a trading career for him, with profits increasing at a steady rate. The losses he incurred along the way appear to be contained, a sign of healthy risk management. Toward the end of the graph he peaks his profits at about $50,000 before getting whipsawed down to $25,000 in a short period of time to close the year with a $1,000 gain, or a little over 4 percent.

In the end he made some money, paid some taxes, and

Leverage

probably learned some lessons. By 2019 his numbness had increased along with his boldness. Determined to take another crack at the markets, he made a series of high-profile posts over a period of two weeks in which he detailed a stomach-churning roller-coaster ride on the FD express, which made his previous year's trading history look like a ride on Disney's It's a Small World.

Rectalcropper2 kept a low profile during most of 2019 and then reemerged during the summer with a screenshot of an all-in bet that had paid off handsomely. He uploaded a post with the title "ALGN Play: 80k Profit in 5 Minutes." He was back in business. In the comments, he expressed his affinity for FDs.

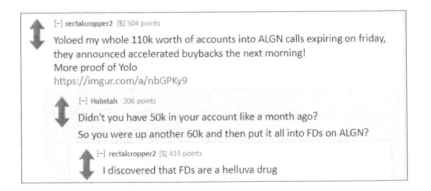

A day later he did it again, with greater profits and even less time—"SPY Puts: 277k Profit in 1 Minute." And with that trade, the self-proclaimed FDholic was worth three-quarters of a million dollars. Rectalcopper2, a college student, had taken a $50,000 account and turned it into $750,000 in a matter of weeks.

Lessons learned from his previous year's adventure were put to good use. Or so he thought. Rectalcopper2 made three more trades before closing out his trading year in 2019.

What happens next is best summarized by Rectalcopper2's comments as well as an account-equity chart estimate, pieced together from his comment history.

[-] rectalcropper2 [S] 697 points
My high a week ago was 750k lmao, now im down 50%. Guess I learned what a parabola is

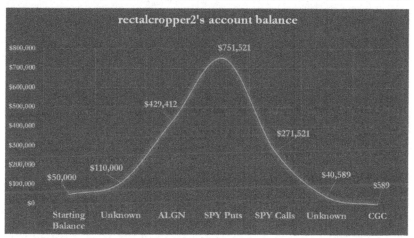

With only three quick trades, he gave the money back to the house. Rectalcopper2's extravagant trades made him the simultaneous winner of both *Most Gains from a Single Play* and *Loss of the Year* in WSB's 2019 Annual Awards.

His experience drew a lot of attention from the subreddit and evoked an unusually irritated sentiment by the community for having lost his fortune. People post wins and losses on a regular

Leverage

basis on WallStreetBets; both are equally welcomed, and both are well received. Typical feedback when someone posts a large win is quite sensible—members encourage the winner to walk away. When losses are posted, they reply with sincere empathy and attempt to comfort the trader with uplifting or humorous comments.

Instead, I believe Rectalcropper2's spectacular experience subconsciously sparked an unspoken ethos of the millennial generation. The motivations behind people on WSB are rarely talked about. They clearly enjoy making money and aren't averse to losing it. It's common for them to make fun of themselves and use sarcasm to rationalize some of the outlandish behavior that takes place, but it's rare to read honest conversations about what drives them.

 [-] Sandvicheater 79 points 21 days ago

Rectalcropper still pisses me off and it's not even my money.

This fuck nugget could've been set for life living off dividends and interest and he yolo a FD lottery ticket.

Shit even the degenerates of this sub was screaming at him to walk away.

In terms of percentage, Rectalcropper2's gains were nothing special—but the amount of money he made was. When people make ten, twenty, fifty, or even a hundred thousand dollars, the community is unphased, and feedback remains lighthearted. But $750,000 is *a lot* of money. Potentially life changing.

Rectalcropper2 crossed some sort of threshold with those profits, which made him different than the rest. Perhaps underneath it all, millennials have a goal to take Wall Street seriously and to use it as a realistic source of low-risk income— but are using high-risk strategies as a viable path to get there (as was the case with TheTriviaTribe). After all, low-interest and dividend-paying portfolios require sizeable capital to have a meaningful impact.

LESSONS LEARNED

Stock options can be extremely dangerous in the hands of novices and powerful if used in certain ways. On different scales, CrystalBaller and flipper321 showed the possible dangers, to both themselves and their brokers, of using options by experimenting with these tools without fully understanding them. The stories of both TheTriviaTribe and rectalcropper2 outline how they can provide incredible leverage that results in attractive payoffs that rival those of casino games. They also show how the behavior displayed by both of these young risk takers resembles that of recreational casino enthusiasts, from the disciplined that can walk away to those that seek the bigger rush and are not able to do the same.

For now, stock options present the most attractive form of leverage, but in an ever-changing and innovative world of financial derivatives, the universe of available tools for

Leverage

speculating could expand. Swaps (currency, credit default, etc...), for example, which provide similar leverage and are currently used *over the counter* (roughly translated to over the phone) by big banks, could make their way into the hands of retail traders under the guise of increased liquidity, availability, or market efficiency and become accessible on these zero-commission platforms for use on WallStreetBets.

5. Charles Schwab, Meet Candy Crush

That's how NBC described the amalgamation between the gamified experience of easy-to-use, app-based brokers and the millennials who use them in the 2019 article "Designed to Distract: Stock app Robinhood nudges users to take risks" by

Charles Schwab, Meet Candy Crush

David Ingram.

When smartphone owners pull up Robinhood's investment app, they're greeted with a variety of dazzling touches: bursts of confetti to celebrate transactions, the price of Bitcoin in neon pink and a list of popular stocks to trade.

He continues:

Rather than directing users to adopt a coherent strategy, the app pushes riskier options...

That pun was probably not intended.

...like individual stocks and cryptocurrencies—and even offers trading on borrowed money, known as margin, and options trading, both of which are used by advanced investors but carry extreme risk.

I disagree. The problem doesn't lie with an app's colors or which stocks it recommends. People deserve more credit than they get when people assume they'll be tempted into switching their retirement funds to Bitcoin just because it's higher on the list when they first sign into their broker.

Trying to figure out why people engage in risky behavior, or why people go to casinos, is beyond the scope of this book.

Perhaps because of the dream of reaching financial independence. After all, the types of trades people take on WallStreetBets have better odds than the Powerball lottery, which is played by millions on a regular basis in the United States (although the size of the trades versus the price of lottery tickets is a different story). Or maybe it's the thrill. Red Bull created an entire industry of daredevils whose careers are defined by living on the edge and performing death-defying stunts.

Whatever the reasons are for people's risky behavior, blaming the broker's interface for encouraging people to use their platform as a slot machine makes for a lazy or, at the least, incomplete argument.

 [−] Low On Coffee 30 points

I feel this. Just switched from RH to TD AmeriSchwab and my gains arent as satisfying in TOS. Besides, all those useful tools, fast deposits, secure trading shit...doesnt give me the same rush as using a fly-by-night brogrammed app.

permalink   embed   unsave   spam   remove   report   give award   reply

However, there is something to be said about the gamification found in all aspects of life in the minds of millennials.

CHEAT CODES

There's nothing new about people or groups of people

Charles Schwab, Meet Candy Crush

65

looking for tricks to make money. In 2009, Terry Herbert found the Staffordshire Hoard, a treasure worth $4.1 million while using a metal detector on a plowed field. In 1993, a group of students, dubbed the Blackjack Team, from the Massachusetts Institute of Technology (MIT) figured out how to beat blackjack at casinos by counting cards. In 1998, Renaissance Technologies established the Medallion Fund, one of the most famous and successful quantitative funds, using what equates to fancy math to beat the market.

But let's be fair, finding treasures, memorizing decks of cards, and beating markets using math is hard. And with each of those examples (and many more), the stated goal is first to make money using some established method and then to work to find and implement the solution.

Millennials have a different approach—they're aware that inefficiencies and opportunities exist everywhere in life, not just money, and try to find a way to work them in their favor. They call these *lifehacks*.

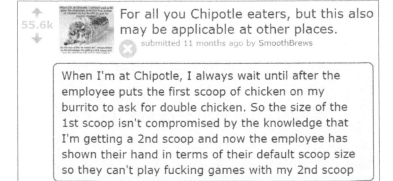

For all you Chipotle eaters, but this also may be applicable at other places.
submitted 11 months ago by SmoothBrews

When I'm at Chipotle, I always wait until after the employee puts the first scoop of chicken on my burrito to ask for double chicken. So the size of the 1st scoop isn't compromised by the knowledge that I'm getting a 2nd scoop and now the employee has shown their hand in terms of their default scoop size so they can't play fucking games with my 2nd scoop

So I was at a Wendys today... (self.wallstreetbets)
submitted by Yottahz to r/wallstreetbets

This was an expensive Wendys in Flagstaff, AZ. How expensive? Well a single was $5.99 for the sandwich only and $9 for the value meal.

The strange thing is, they had the 2 for $5 deal and one of the items you could buy was Dave's single (one of the other was 10 tendies)

So a person who is not so hungry and doesn't like to waste food would pay $5.99 for a single while a a*** would go for the 2 for $5 and get a single and the ten tendies and just toss the tendies, saving $1 that they could later YOLO on Tesla 420s.

It fucked me up so much in the head that I asked for an option on a Frosty.

They're also tech savvy; lots of them play video games. For those who have, their minds have been molded from a young age to beat bosses and find secret passageways and bonus levels. And that's how they view the world—things are games that can be beat, optimal strategies that can be used, and cheat codes that can be found.

It's only logical they try to find ways to save or even make them money. Tons of websites and forums exist, dedicated to sharing hacks for online discount offers, rebate programs, or other promotions that have loopholes that were overlooked. On WSB it's no different.

Here's a snippet of someone who thinks he beat the sports gambling system:

Charles Schwab, Meet Candy Crush

Here's one that figured out a (flawed) credit card cash-back strategy:

Can you buy stock with a credit card?
submitted by the_thou_factor (self.wallstreetbets)
69 comments   share   save   hide   report

If so. You can get infinite money.

Step 1. Buy a safe stock with a credit card that gets 2% cash back. (not the usual WSB move but it's for infinite trendies so it's worth it)

Step 2. Sell the stock.

Step 3. Use the cash to pay off the credit card.

Step 4. Repeat

You could get 2% growth every at least every week with this. Millionaire in 5 years easy.

And my personal favorite. This was not posted publicly but as a private message to the WallStreetBets moderator team. This clever kid tried to leverage WSB to cheat his way into Harvard. It's not free money, but had his strategy worked, it would have certainly paid off:

wallstreetbets •

Lemme own this subreddit so I can get into Harvard.

u/I_LIKE_CHEAT_CODES

Nothing will look better on my essay to get into Harvard than owning this.
Let me borrow this subreddit until 2022 lmao?

u/WilliamNyeTho

Like you want to buy shares?

u/I_LIKE_CHEAT_CODES

Ok so I saw this post on a Harvard forum saying they owned a mediocre
finance website and they got accepted into Harvard with slightly above
average grades.

I was just tryn to ask if I could become some type of "owner". It doesn't
even have to be a real role just something I could prove.

And no, we did not let him own the subreddit or help him cheat his way into Harvard in any way.[10]

Outside of WallStreetBets, a young trader named Navinder Sarao from the UK got in trouble with the law after making over $70 million from his parent's basement (more on him in Chapter 10). He later described to authorities that his true motivation was the thrill of winning a video game. From an article on BBC titled *Hounslow trader avoids jail in 'flash crash' case*:

---

[10] Harvard, in case you're reading this, for the good of the country, I recommend you accept the people who own r/finance long before accepting those who own r/wallstreetbets.

Charles Schwab, Meet Candy Crush

Mr Burlingame said that Mr Sarao almost believed he was playing a highly sophisticated and complicated video game and he affectively found the best "cheat" to win the game.

PDT

As accessible as gambling on Walls Street is to retail traders, there is one rule that acts as an effective speed bump to those with smaller accounts. This rule is known as the Pattern Day Trading rule (or PDT). According to FINRA's website:

The primary purpose of the day-trading margin rules is to require that certain levels of equity be deposited and maintained in day-trading accounts, and that these levels be sufficient to support the risks associated with day-trading activities. It was determined that the prior day-trading margin rules did not adequately address the risks inherent in certain patterns of day trading and had encouraged practices, such as the use of cross-guarantees, that **did not require customers to demonstrate actual financial ability to engage in day trading** [emphasis added].

FINRA states this rule as "any margin customer that day trades (buys then sells or sells short then buys the same security on the same day) four or more times in five business days [...] must maintain minimum equity of $25,000 on any day that the customer day trades." In other words, anyone who wants to day trade (buy and sell frequently) needs to have a decent sized account. Traders who don't meet the minimum requirements are quick to find out that their brokers are efficient with enforcing this rule and therefore in constant search for work-arounds to this restriction. In this case enforcement requires either depositing enough to meet the minimum equity or facing a ninety-day suspension from any trading so that the violator can think hard about what he has done. People's creativity to circumvent these rules knows no bounds.

The first, obvious attempt is to organize a movement to make changes to the regulation.

Charles Schwab, Meet Candy Crush

change.org

Repeal the Pattern Day Trader rule

The Pattern Day Trader rule (PDT) is an unconstitutional law which states any person with under $25,000 may not place more than 3 day trades per week when purchasing stock while using a margin account. This rule's supposed intent was to prevent new

When these attempts prove unsuccessful, users turn to filing complaints with their legislators and directly with the US Securities and Exchange Commission (SEC):

PDT: It's my money and I need to gamble it away now!
submitted 8 to r/wallstreetbets

If I think a law is as dumb as the Pattern Day Trader rule, I call/email my senator/mayor/big cheese. However, I'm not sure if there's a formal process for the SEC since its different. There have been a few petitions on shit like change.org but of course that goes nowhere. I saw a few complaint filing pages on sec.gov but they're all against a specific company.

Anybody ever done this before?

Then there are people who simply don't care about the rules and, out of desperation, decide to break the rule and take their chances:

Robinhood enabled my [stupidity] by allowing me to ignore the Pattern Day Trader Rule! Can you do it too?
submitted 1 month ago * by widowkiller to r/wallstreetbets

50

So trump tweets pumped up my puts a few weeks back. I was sitting on some decent cash. If i had been less [of a dumbass], I would have took my money out and been done with it but nooooooo i just HAD to yolo on some more SPY puts. Of course, I couldn't properly time jack shit and i end up with 30% of my portfolio gone. In my fit of a******* screeching, i realized I used up all my day trades. So i decided "you know what, im doing one more trade, getting restricted, and then im out of this fucking game until i pay off these [stupid] loans of mine"

Of course, I fucked that trade too, and during my next bout of rage I also somehow continued to trade in a daze. next thing I know, i've made 12 more fucking random put and call buys! now my account is down 70 goddamn percent! This is not freaking normal, is it?!

More to the point, why did this goddamn platform enable a disabled person to day trade beyond the pattern day trader rule? This was on friday, and now today im properly restricted. Someone get me in touch with cnbc, all aspiring [gamblers] need to spam day trades on their final day!

In fact, if the stated purposes of the PDT rules were to "support the risk" associated with, or to demonstrate the financial ability to engage in, day trading, they may have unintentionally had the opposite effect.

PDT [sucks] (self.wallstreetbets)
submitted 1 month ago to r/wallstreetbets

24

Title says it all, I know I'm going to be restricted by tomorrow, so anyone have any longer term play since I'll only be able to close positions? Either that or I'm tempted to nuke my account/FD to 25k

Charles Schwab, Meet Candy Crush

The most common way for traders who don't have the $25,000 in their accounts to get around the PDT rules is to simply open multiple broker accounts.

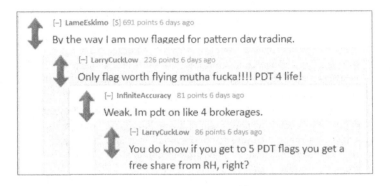

[-] LameEskimo [S] 691 points 6 days ago
By the way I am now flagged for pattern day trading.

    [-] LarryCuckLow 226 points 6 days ago
    Only flag worth flying mutha fucka!!!! PDT 4 life!

        [-] InfiniteAccuracy 81 points 6 days ago
        Weak. Im pdt on like 4 brokerages.

            [-] LarryCuckLow 86 points 6 days ago
            You do know if you get to 5 PDT flags you get a free share from RH, right?

In the end, the efficacy of these rules is debatable, as people have demonstrated their ability to intentionally ignore or find ways around the rules by trading more than they should with small accounts. It's also unclear how having large accounts would help traders "demonstrate" people's financial ability to engage in day trading.

FREE MONEY

Risks associated with trading aren't exclusive to the traders but in many cases to the brokers as well. A prime example would be the case of flipper321 where, although things worked out in everyone's favor, things could have been disastrous. The day he exited his position for a six-figure profit ended up having a market drop—which could have resulted in an $800,000 loss if handled improperly. It is up to the broker to implement the necessary risk controls to protect itself against situations in which customers owe more money than they deposited in their accounts.

In most cases brokers do a good job at preventing trading accounts from ever ending up with negative balances. This is done by identifying potential trades which can go negative and securing the necessary collateral for the duration of the trades. In cases where account equity crosses predefined thresholds, positions are closed out automatically. The same goes with certain types of options trades that carry special kinds of risks.

At the same time, the brokerage industry is growing at a fast pace, and start-ups eager to innovate are joining an increasingly crowded market space while offering attractive products to set themselves apart. Meanwhile, traders and investors welcome competition as brokers fighting for market share make these brokers easier and cheaper to use. With this (or any) growth comes the risk of making mistakes. One such mistake was found and exploited in a high-profile way on WallStreetBets toward the end of 2019.

WSB user ShapeTheMessaging (commonly referred to as STM) signed up for margin on his trading account, which basically means his broker will loan him twice his money to trade with for a small fee. This is extremely common and has been offered by practically all brokers since the beginning of time.

Charles Schwab, Meet Candy Crush

STM deposited $2,000 in his account, and with his margin he had the ability to buy twice that amount in stocks or options. He then purchased one hundred shares worth of stocks, which cost him almost $4,000, and then *sold* a certain type of *covered call.* Remember options can both be bought and sold by people, so in this case STM was on the other side of a bet that someone made that the stocks would go up. As collateral for selling the "bet," he used the shares. The price of the option he sold was roughly $4,000.

At this point, STM was basically in a neutral situation. He owned shares that would make him money if they went up, but he made a bet with someone by selling an option that would lose money if those same shares went up. In other words, it was hard for him to either make or lose money. Most brokers would have realized that all his capital was tied up in an apparently senseless trade and blocked him from making other trades unless he either deposited more money or closed out his existing trade. Instead his broker mistakenly took the $4,000 from the call option STM sold as a new deposit in his account and let him use it as he pleased. To make matters worse, because he had signed up for margin, his buying power was now *twice* that amount (or nearly $8,000). He doubled his buying power again.

So, what did STM do? He bought more shares, sold more covered calls, got more money, and doubled up again. Then again. And then again. By the time he stopped, his initial $2,000 deposit had given him over $50,000 worth of buying power.

Then with this buying power in his account, he thought it sensible to use it to go all in with FDs that expired the next day using Apple, which had its quarterly earning reports due that Thursday evening.

On Friday morning STM streamed his spectacular loss on YouTube and registered well over a million views.

Over the weekend WallStreetBets was filled with chatter and commentary over this fearless display of risk. Unlike usual high-risk traders who risk their own capital, STM ended up with a negative account balance of over $50,000. This astounding level of personal-risk tolerance had never been seen before.

By Monday morning eager WSBers were astonished to find that this glitch had not been fixed by the broker yet, and so it became a race to use the same technique in hopes to get rich quick.

After all, had STM picked calls instead of puts (or had Apple's price gone the other way) his profits would have paid off handsomely. If people used this same approach with even greater leverage, they could surely turn into millionaires overnight. It didn't take long before the first user reached $1 million worth of buying power.

Robinhood free money cheat works pretty well. 1 million dollar position on 4k
submitted to r/wallstreetbets

Charles Schwab, Meet Candy Crush

By November 5, there was a post on WSB labeled "GUH of Fame 2019," which listed users who had taken the most outrageous positions. In the description, it read, "To celebrate our new Infinite Money Cheat Code, it is only fair that we honor the autists that brought it to us, and thoroughly explored it for us all," and included the following chart:

Rank	Leveraged	Deposited	Gain/Loss	Link
GUHlumbus	$48,000	$2,000	Uncertain	Post
dos commas	$1,300,000	$15,000	-$190,000	Post
dos commas	$1,279,550	$4,000	~$400	Post
Autist	$314,070	$5,000	~$5,000	Post
arGUHmedes	$1,732,640	$3,000	TBD	Post - archived

This event garnered so much media attention that this broker was able to identify users that were abusing this glitch and start freezing users' accounts before they could use their massive buying power on other YOLOs.

At the time it remained unclear who would be responsible for the losses in the event of negative balances. There is little precedent in these situations, as brokers typically prevent these situations relatively well. Josh Brown suggested on CNBC that "if one of these kids blows up an account, these kids aren't going to make a margin call for a million dollars."

A few days after, media reports started surfacing with leaked memos from users, which showed the brokers were canceling accounts and demanding repayment of any money that was lost within sixty days.

Bloomberg reported on November 7, 2019, that this event ended up resulting in $100,000 worth of losses, with around twenty accounts being involved.

≡ **Bloomberg**

Technology

Robinhood Is Back in Washington's Crosshairs After Leverage Glitch

By Matt Robinson and Julie Verhage
November 7, 2019, 12:35 PM EST

▶ Flaw said to involve about 20 accounts and $100,000 in losses

▶ Regulators are asking what led to 'infinite leverage' trades

---

For millennials, life is just one big software development life cycle. Rules or parameters are set by governments, organizations, businesses, or social norms. Once deployed, millions of users find a way to test them out in real time in search for bugs.

Finance is complicated, and the broker business is even more

Charles Schwab, Meet Candy Crush

so. Developing a platform for masses to use runs inadvertent risks like the one exploited by the infinite margin glitch, as well as predefined risks, such as those seen in situations like the one flipper321 founds himself in.

The kinds of risks imposed on brokers when people stumble on and take advantage of cheat codes could be contained if they were limited to isolated cases. They become much more difficult when large groups of people make it their goal to hunt for and capitalize on exploitable weaknesses. Not to mention share them on social media to make them go viral.

To my knowledge, brokers haven't had the proper stress tests to withstand stampedes of high-risk thumb traders that aren't afraid of margin calls.[11]

[−] Hadron90 149 points 1 month ago ✔
Sign up with a boomer broker if you want to trade stocks or commodities or real estate or whatever you old fucks trade. Robinhood is for millenials who trade options and zoomers who trade crypto. I heard Robinhood won't even give you an account if you are over 30 years old.

---

[11] Margin calls are like speeding tickets for traders. They're issued when someone crossed a line with risk, which in turn requires them to pony up more cash in their account as collateral to make up for bad behavior.

6. Tools

The only thing more dangerous than thrill-seeking millennials armed with normal stock options is thrill-seeking millennials armed with options on leveraged, synthetic, inversed, thrice-removed financial derivatives known as Exchange Traded Funds (ETF).

ETFs are big. Like very, very big. "U.S.-based exchange-traded funds have racked up a record $4 trillion in assets under management as of this year, with 136 ETF providers offering 2,062 ETFs to investors," according to CNBC's Lizzy Gurdus. To put that in context, that's almost as much as Japan's annual GDP—and Japan has the world's third-largest economy. That's as much as Canada and Mexico put together.

Deborah Fuhr, founder of ETFGI and a leading expert on the ETF industry, said, "Today, the ETF industry globally is $2.5 trillion bigger than the hedge fund industry. [...] The top 10 ETFs trading on U.S. exchanges account for 28% of total U.S.

Tools

assets under management, with the top 20 U.S. ETFs accounting for nearly 40% of assets in the space."

FUN AND EASY

First, for the purposes of simplicity, I'm grouping Exchange Traded Funds (ETFs) with Exchange Traded Notes (ETNs) and Exchange Traded Products (ETPs). Since the most commonly (albeit sometimes incorrectly) used acronym is ETF, I'll be using that one. There are important structural differences between them, just not any that are relevant here.

In its purist form, an ETF is a basket of stocks, bundled and packaged up under its own ticker symbol and sold it as if it were a normal stock. A popular example is an ETF with the symbol SPY, which replicates the S&P 500 index and allows investors to simply buy shares of it and replicate its performance without the need for hiring an investment fund. This is similar to one of the two investments (referenced at the beginning at the book) TossOut5451 held onto for a decade to make $1.7 million.

A more generic description for them is stocks that mimic the price of other things. Some of the things they mimic are real, tangible goods like oil, gold, and silver. Others are so abstract that they can only be described as the wasteful byproduct of a mathematician's bad acid trip.

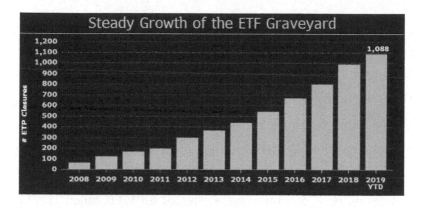

Steady Growth of the ETF Graveyard

There are ETFs that are safe, legitimate assets, which serve as serious investment vehicles, even ones that pay dividends. These are immensely popular for all the right reasons—they provide low-cost alternative investment routes for people looking to invest in the markets without hiring separate investment banks or hedge funds. However, the ETFs primarily discussed here are not; they are just fancy toys. They're a complex orchestration of maneuvers made frequently behind the scenes between issuers, counterparties, and market exchanges that masquerade as innocuous stocks for kids to gamble with from their phones.

Will you be getting into the ETF ETF? (self.wallstreetbets)
submitted 2 years ago by SovietWarfare to r/wallstreetbets

There is now an ETF for ETFs, it's called $TETF. Way to go guys, now we can lose money at twice as fast!

Let's start with a simple example.

If a trader wants to dabble with crude oil, ETFs can be quite

Tools

practical. Say she thinks the price of oil is going to go up, she can buy futures. In theory, futures would give her the exposure she's looking for, and in fact she could even end up with a basement full of fifty-five-gallon drums of flammable liquid. Of course, this requires having a broker with access to futures, getting approval for trading them, meeting margin requirements, paying commissions, having a big basement, etc. Or she can just opt for buying, without commissions, shares of an ETF called UWTI, which tracks the price of oil. Actually, in the case of UWTI, it pays two-to-one leverage for extra fun (meaning, if the price of oil increases by 1 percent, the ETF increases by 2 percent or vice versa in the case of a loss). This is possible because the issuer of the ETF makes trades behind the scenes, using futures or other means, to try and replicate the price of oil on behalf of the customers who buy UWTI. The issuer is the one that needs to worry about the margin requirements and fancy trades and in some cases physical storage logistics while being able to provide a seamless experience to buyers of the ETF who just want to bet on oil prices.

Will Hershey, a cofounder of independent ETF-issuer Roundhill Investments and an occasional visitor of

WallStreetBets broke down ETFs into the following categories: Passive, Active, Equity, Fixed Income, Commodity, Asset Allocation, Alternative, Volatility, Currency, and possibly Cryptocurrency ETFs in the near future.

Other popular examples are when ETF issuers combine these hard-to-trade securities and bundle them up into fun thematic packages. Some are quite creative:

- VMBS—Mortgage backed security ETF for those who felt left out of the 2008 banking collapse because MBSs were not available for retail investors at the time. Now millennials don't need to feel left out.

- SHE—Holds firms of US companies with a high proportion of women in leadership positions.

- BJK—(A play on Blackjack) Literally a casino ETF.

- WSKY—Whiskey.

- FPX—Invests in initial public offerings (IPOs). Or simply put companies going public, regardless of their sector, size, or profitability, even WeWork.

- YINN and YANG—triple-leveraged bull and bear China ETFs.

- CURE and SICK—triple-leveraged bull and bear health-care ETFs.

- GCE—It's like the black box of ETFs. It invests in other funds without telling you which. The issuer (Goldman Sachs) doesn't provide a working website for investors to access in order to learn what this thing does. As of the

Tools

writing of this book, it's up 23 percent year to date.

Life Settlement Investing: How to profit off the death of baby boomers.

submitted by StevenMcphearson to r/wallstreetbets

There's two constants in this universe. Death and taxes.

I'm gonna explain using emojis since I don't think any of you had proper sex ed before.

Everybody croaks. So what do we do? We buy life insurance and if we GUH'd that money goes to someone. Not everyone has someone, so there's a thing called life settlements. Instead of hoarding that cash, when nobody will even use it, you take it out. Investors are banking on you to die eventually.

https://partners4prosperity.com/life-settlement-investments-pros-and-cons-facts-faqs/

So who's coming up for their rendezvous with death? Boomers.

[–] astroyeet 17 points

No ETFs? I feel like there's an ETF for everything these days

WHAT'S IN A NAME?

You may have noticed that the names some of these ETFs use to trade with are fun, and they are. Marketing is the oldest trick in the book—and it turns out Wall Street is not immune to it. Trends suggest that people collectively trust their retirement and pension funds in companies with cute names over other, possibly more serious, metrics.

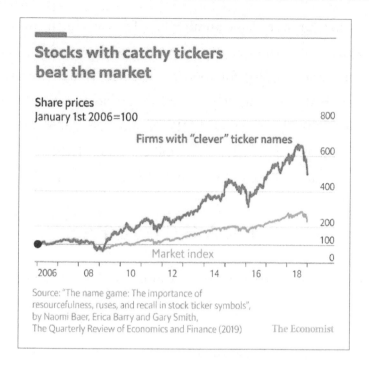

Stocks with catchy tickers beat the market

Share prices
January 1st 2006=100

Firms with "clever" ticker names

Market index

Source: "The name game: The importance of resourcefulness, ruses, and recall in stock ticker symbols", by Naomi Baer, Erica Barry and Gary Smith, The Quarterly Review of Economics and Finance (2019)

The Economist

A study made at Pomona College in 2019 compared the performance of stocks with "clever" ticker symbols against the overall market and found that, in all cases, they outperformed the market by significant margins—giving Efficient Market Hypothesis (EMH)[12] evangelists something to think about. The result of this study simultaneously ridicules professional analysts, who dedicate their lives to breaking down spreadsheets and producing elaborate investment reports, and reinforces the mind-set millennials have that Wall Street isn't serious. It could

---

[12] In economics, EMH states that the market tends to be efficient and prices tend to reflect all publicly available information in a rational manner.

Tools

also help explain the large number of ETFs with catchy tickers.

Some additional examples include: GAMR for video games, MJ for marijuana, PBJ for food & beverage, HACK for cyber security, BARN for farming, BLNG for precious metals, CARZ for cars, COW for livestock, FOIL for pure aluminum, MONY for financials sector, RING for miners fund, TAN for solar, WOOD and CUT for timber and forest, and many, many more.

LEVERAGED ETFS

In addition to providing easy exposure to things that are hard to trade, ETFs have an additional feature that makes them appealing: leverage.

Understanding leveraged ETFs is simple at face value but complex behind the scenes. Simply put, they give you magnified returns (for either wins or losses) on whatever it is they are tracking. In other words, a leveraged ETF that tracks the S&P promises to replicate in the short term whatever it is the index does with double or triple returns. In fact, the SEC recently approved a quadruple-leveraged ETF. Investors and traders alike can get this additional exposure without needing to have special margin requirements in their account or applying for special account privileges. They simply search for the ETF symbol and buy the shares as if they were regular stocks. Someone, somewhere, has to worry about the hocus-pocus to generate the magnified returns that are promised.

Summary
- On Tuesday, the SEC approved the first 4x leveraged ETFs.
- The new ETFs will track 4x or -4x the daily performance of the S&P 500.
- Given the pitfalls of holding leveraged ETFs over time, investors should only use these funds for short-term trading application.

However, due to these behind-the-scenes complexities, these securities tend to have quirks that often times go ignored by new traders or investors who are lured by the promise of big gains. For example, both long (bull) and short (bear) leveraged ETFs have a nasty long-term side effect of going to zero dollars in choppy markets (when the markets bounce up and down) regardless of what the underlying asset does. They can also have the opposite effect in trending markets (when the markets go up in a straight line); that is they compound. Since 2008, markets have gone up in a relatively straight line, so many millennials and new investors have no idea ETFs have this property. I suspect they will find out the hard way the next time the markets experience actual volatility.

INVERSED ETFS

If and when markets experience a downturn, this same

Tools

demographic of traders and investors can also turn to other types of ETFs to give them ways to easily benefit from collapsing prices.

Typically, if a trader wanted to make money from declining prices, she would engage in short selling. This is a way of betting on prices going down instead of up. However, short selling is not as easy as buying stocks (or betting prices will go up). Some brokers don't offer the ability to do this, and the brokers that do offer it require special account permissions, which often include additional account deposits. In some cases, even if people meet all the criteria, it is still impossible to short certain stocks for other technical reasons.

Inverse ETFs fix all this. Once again, ETF issuers find a way, behind the scenes, to wheel and deal their way into replicating short sales of all sorts things.

How are inverse funds like $SH not the antidote to a recession or depression?
submitted by 2ook to r/wallstreetbets

I just found out about inverse funds a couple minutes ago. They literally do the opposite of what their counterpart does. Why can't people in a bear market just buy these inverse funds and receive bull market returns? I used to be worried about a recession or market crash, but now 6i know I can just buy these funds and eventually go long on a 3x spy etf at the bottom. I recommend you do the same.

Hahahahahahahaha How The Fuck Is The Great Depression Real Hahahaha Just Buy An Inverse Fund

In fact, WSB even suggests the use of ETFs as a work-around

(or "cheat code") for people who have restrictions on short selling to use with their retirement funds.

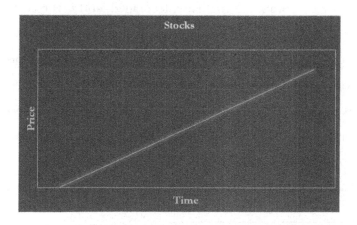

 Bad or Absolutely Genius: Boomers should just buy Inverse ETFs and hold until the next financial collapse.
submitted 10 months ago by Question-Asking_Prof to r/wallstreetbets

- The theory here is that there are a ton of boomers out there with fat IRAs.
- Short-selling is not allowed in an IRA.
- But the markets are inevitably going to correct before their retirement. (*assumption*)
- They don't want to lose all kind of money and potential Harley Davidsons.
- So they pack their portfolios with inverse ETFs so they profit when the market declines.

The reason why it's more difficult for brokers to allow short selling is simple: it's riskier than buying stocks. In the long term, the stock market's prices have historically gone up, with no apparent end in sight.

In theory, if someone were to buy stocks (or bet that stocks Tools are going up), they would be facing unlimited potential gains while facing limited risk. That is, they could only lose 100 percent of their investment if the stock price fell to zero dollars. On the flip side, if they were short selling, they would be facing *unlimited risk* if they held on to their losing bet and the stocks continued climbing forever. For this reason, brokers take additional precautions to protect themselves against risky traders potentially ending up with negative balances. Some don't allow this at all.

WHO ABSORBS THE RISKS?

ETFs have another wonderful property. Unlike normal companies, which have a defined number of outstanding shares,[13] ETF issuers can magically create new shares on demand as needed.

There are combined thematic, leveraged, and inversed ETFs with humorously named ticker symbols that—because they trade like normal stocks—also come with stock options. Millions of kids can use their commission-free broker and free money cheat codes to make large FD bets to short "health care" by buying call options on the triple-leveraged inverse SICK ETF (buying call options because SICK ETF is inverse). They could alternatively buy put options on CURE. They can get assigned

---

[13] Outstanding shares are the number of shares publicly available for people to buy.

without understanding why, like flipper321 did with his $23 million in shares, and the ETF issuer would have to produce them out of thin air if they're not available.

At this point, sound economists reading this must be scratching their heads and wondering to themselves: who absorbs the risks here? If brokers make it difficult or even prevent short selling altogether because it's too risky and these ETFs somehow circumvent restrictions, then how is this asymmetry explained?

Somebody somewhere is absorbing infinite risk times three, for every inverse triple-leveraged ETF share it creates. And it creates unlimited shares if enough people want them.

In the end it doesn't matter. These things are fun, the prices move up and down a lot, and the grown-ups have most likely figured it all out. Besides, just because things are complicated, doesn't mean they pose systemic risks.

Meanwhile, the SEC recently passed a rule to "modernize regulation of exchange-traded funds" to make it easier for ETFs to be created, with the hope that competition will give investors more attractive choices to pick from.

Since I created WSB nearly eight years ago, not a single month has gone by without somebody making a post recommending an ETF be made specifically for the subreddit.

279 Lets make a WSB ETF for 2020 (self.wallstreetbets)
submitted by Ardesic53 to r/wallstreetbets

Tools

93

7. Systemic Risks

At the age of twenty, WSB member Biglanna completed his compulsory service with the Singapore military back in 2015 and began laying down the groundwork for his professional career in the stock market. He started with about $20,000, which he had saved from his time in the military, plus around $30,000 from an inheritance. He taught himself the ins and outs of the stock market from free online sites like Khan Academy and Reddit, taking particular interest in volatility instruments. Impressively, he took the combined $50,000 and amassed an eye-popping $4 million in just three years.[14] This was not done through the typical YOLO trades seen on WSB but rather a diligent trading strategy and a deep understanding of the quirks of the volatility products he used.

---

[14] By 2018 his trading account was actually bigger than $4 million due to investments he had accepted from friends and family.

Experienced traders know that in order to be consistently profitable, trading strategies need proper risk management as well as a positive expected value from any given trade. In other words, it's OK to lose some trades and win others as long as the end result nets positive. Experienced traders rely on statistical models that can predict expected outcomes based on averages, which in turn are derived from measuring stuff that happens on a regular basis. But every so often, very improbable (or statistically impossible) things happen, and such profitable systems break down. Nassim Taleb, a former options trader turned statistical philosopher, coined the term for such events as *black swans.*

On February 5, 2018, a black swan event hit Wall Street. After the markets experienced volatility levels not seen since 1987, Biglanna made a post on WallStreetBets showing a $4.3 million loss. The majority thanks to a single ETF he was holding called XIV.

Systemic Risks

The unraveling of XIV was fast and violent. On Friday February 2, it had a closing price of around $115. By the following Monday, it closed at $99. One day later, $7. Two weeks after that, the ETF was liquidated by its issuer Credit Suisse, and any investors who had bought into XIV prior to February lost over 95 percent of their investment, with no chance of recovering it.

The events surrounding the collapse of this ETF were remarkable, complex, and extremely unique. XIV along with other similar ETFs not only suffered similar losses, but they managed to cause ripple effects across the entire financial system. These instruments sparked investigations and drew criticisms, which may have played a role in the way of self-propagating feedback loops. They exposed a tangible example of a systemic risk which academics had been warning about as only hypothetical up until that day. In order to explain what happened on this day, I'll break down the various components and piece them all together at the end.

THE VIX

You may have noticed VIX is XIV (what Biglanna traded) spelled backward; that is not a coincidence. It's another example of an ETF with a cute name. The VIX is the Chicago Board of Exchange Volatility Index, which for practical purposes is a number that tends to go up when the markets go down and vice versa. It's why they affectionately call it the *fear index* on TV. Since fear is hard to quantify, the VIX relies on this simple formula to come up with its value instead:

$$\sigma^2 = \tfrac{2}{T} \sum_i \tfrac{\Delta K_i}{K_i^2} e^{RT} Q(K_i) - \tfrac{1}{T}\left[\tfrac{F}{K_0} - 1\right]^2$$

WallStreetBets user joeyrb tried explaining this formula in a comment thread, which for some reason later ended up quoted on Bloomberg:

> VIX is an average of [implied volatility] on an [out of the money] sample of rolling 30 day [S&P 500] options meant to represent what the implied 12 month 1 standard deviation move is for the [S&P 500]

Systemic Risks

In other words, the easy-to-understand fear index is quite abstract under the hood. But it has another important property that is hard to ignore: WSB and others think it's fun to trade. When the VIX moves, it moves a lot, giving day traders plenty of action to work with. It also has predictive qualities, which make it attractive for traders to build profitable strategies around. The problem with the VIX is that it's just a math formula, which by itself cannot be traded. It's an idea computed by measuring a bunch of arbitrary prices.

DERIVATIVES

There are two major categories in finance: underlying assets and derivatives. The first category, underlying assets, is explained as anything that has and defines its own value. This can be a stock, an ounce of gold, an office chair, or a house. The second category is explained as contractual paperwork that surrounds the first category. This includes stock options, futures contracts on gold, a sales agreement for the office chair, or flood insurance for the house. A good rule of thumb to distinguish between the two categories is: if it can be explained to a five-year-old, it's probably an underlying asset. Otherwise it's a derivative. There can also be derivatives of derivatives and so on.

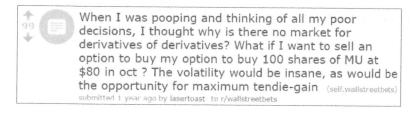

When I was pooping and thinking of all my poor decisions, I thought why is there no market for derivatives of derivatives? What if I want to sell an option to buy my option to buy 100 shares of MU at $80 in oct ? The volatility would be insane, as would be the opportunity for maximum tendie-gain (self.wallstreetbets)
submitted 1 year ago by lasertoast to r/wallstreetbets

Since the VIX is an arbitrary math formula that by itself can't be traded, derivatives were created to allow for this. VIX derivatives include futures, options, and ETFs. Below is a chart that shows the various steps that happen for a VIX ETF to get its final value, where each arrow can be thought of as a derivative. The first box represents an underlying asset from which all other boxes derive their value.

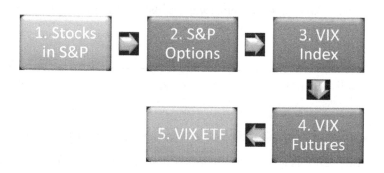

If stock prices in the first box go down, there is a trickle-down effect that works its way across each of the subsequent boxes and, in turn, affects their prices. Under no circumstances should the order of these arrows ever be reversed.

What Biglanna was trading when he lost millions was in the fifth box. XIV is an appropriately named inverse VIX ETF

Systemic Risks

issued by Credit Suisse, and its value is intended to go up whenever the VIX goes down—he was using ETFs to short sell the VIX. Roughly speaking, he expected XIV to increase in value if the market's *fear index* dropped. And the fear index typically drops when the market goes up.

FEBRUARY 5, 2018

Monday was a tough day for indexes but far from record breaking. The S&P posted a 4 percent drop, which, considering the performance it had in prior month, could be chalked up to a fear-inducing correction. The VIX, on the other hand, did break records; for the first time in history, it went up over 100 percent in a single day. Anyone who was bullish with the market had a bad day, but anyone who was short the VIX had an even worse day.

You'll recall from the previous chapter that inverse ETFs allow buyers of these securities to outsource the *unlimited risk* associated with short selling to the issuers. In order to make that possible, ETF issuers need to pull all sorts of tricks. In the case for VIX, inverse ETFs need to short sell futures, but in cases where they lose a lot of money (like they did on February 5), they also need to rebalance their total assets by buying futures as well. These maneuvers done by all ETFs are publicly known and performed daily between four and a quarter past four o'clock in the afternoon.

Halfway through the trading day on this particular Monday, when VIX was skyrocketing, it was apparent that all the inverse VIX ETFs,[15] including Credit Suisse's, would need to buy a lot of futures (box number four in the diagram) when the market closed. Such a strong demand for futures was sure to drive the futures prices up, which created a unique opportunity for profit. When traders everywhere realized this, they decided to jump on this money-making opportunity and bought up a lot of VIX futures before four o'clock in the afternoon with hopes to sell them back to the ETF issuers at a higher price. The result was that VIX futures prices immediately shot up, not because fear was increasing but because traders were trying to front-run money from the ETF issuers. Since the VIX futures shot up, market observers got nervous as a result and decided to buy put options (box number two) and sell stocks and futures for the S&P (box number one). This drove up the VIX (box number three) even further, which then forced ETF issuers to have to buy even more futures. What should have been a one-way trip of prices moving their way sequentially from box one to box five became a round trip. This created a disastrous feedback loop, which wrecked absolute havoc on VIX ETFs. Thanks to box number five, price changes were trickling up to all the previous boxes, which then required changes to trickle back down. Then again, and again, and again—the system broke. On Twitter, this

---

[15] Not only inverse VIX ETFs but also double-leveraged bull ETFs as well.

Systemic Risks

day became known as the great volcalypse. With VIX up over 100 percent, most inverse ETFs had lost nearly all their value that day. Credit Suisse liquidated XIV a few weeks later.

XIV investors lost an estimated total of $1.6 billion that day and later tried suing Credit Suisse to no avail thanks to a surprisingly accurate description of its product on page 197 of its prospectus:

The long term expected value of your ETNs is zero.

This is 100 percent serious.

If you hold your ETNs as a long-term investment, it is likely you will lose all or a substantial portion of your investment.

And with this line buried hundreds of pages deep in the disclosure form, Credit Suisse was absolved of legal responsibility. To the company's credit, volatility ETFs are complicated, and this was not Credit Suisse's first blunder with these products. In 2012, the company made headlines when it halted the creation of double-leveraged VIX ETF shares (TVIX), resulting in all sorts of bizarre things happening across the various interconnected volatility products that exist.

Biglanna's loss was the biggest ever to be recorded on WallStreetBets to date. His post received so much attention that he was eventually contacted by a reputable financial institution that validated his claims about his trading history and offered him a job, where he remains gainfully employed to this day.

TWO WORLDS

Biglanna did not lose $4.3 million because of FDs or YOLOs. He lost the money due to a black swan event caused by the incredibly complex and unforeseeable behavior of layered financial derivatives stacked on top of each other.

What happened this first week of February was a perfect storm between the convolution of these volatility instruments, the devastating feedback loops they cause, knowledgeable traders trying to take advantage of these arbitrage opportunities, and the massive size of the market for them. The VIX index itself cannot be traded; it's just a number, but all the leveraged and inversed ETFs associated with it are easily accessible from commission-free brokerage accounts with the lowest possible risk permissions. Not to mention that stock options are also available on top of these already leveraged derivatives.

In February 2018, shortly after the volcalypse, there was an interesting exchange between Jim Cramer and David Faber on CNBC's *Squawk Box* regarding volatility products and WallStreetBets:

Cramer: UVXY coming back in on heavy buy. We don't want to see that.

Systemic Risks

The symbol he's referring to, UVXY, is a leveraged VIX ETF. He continues.

Cramer: You know, obviously we have to follow the VIX. I hate having to follow these things that are really bogus stocks. But they were created by Wall Street, David. I talked to some people who trade…

Faber: Hey, there are a lot of things that were created by Wall Street. Every single time we have a crisis, we realize all the things Wall Street has created that come back to haunt us.

Cramer: Exactly

Faber: But that's not this; that's not this.

Cramer: David, do you know what Reddit is?

Faber: Reddit?

Cramer: Yeah what kids watch and read. Well one of my friends who trade this says the best article about this was in Reddit. You know who trades this besides all the moron hedge funds? *millennials*! Because it's experiential! It's so exciting! How millennials they like bungee jumping and they like cruises and they like standing in places that we will never go to, and they like playing the double x ultra VIX two-time action because it's *experiential!* They can do it on Instagram! They Instagram themselves doing this, OK? Snap it.

A clear reference to WSB.

Faber: Do you think this experience will have any sort of lesson for them?

Cramer: Yeah that they get the s*it beat out of them, and the next thing you know they're going back, trying go to grad school.

While it is tempting to focus on Cramer's outburst aimed at WSB, it's easy to miss what's behind it. He starts off annoyed by the VIX and not wanting to discuss it. He hints at an important and valid question and then takes his frustration out on Instagram, asking: why are these college kids playing with abstract volatility instruments and straying away from investing in physical companies with potentially value-added benefits? Isn't that what Wall Street is for?

* * *

This was a very challenging chapter to write as trying to simplify the events that took place behind Biglanna's loss is a nearly impossible task. People familiar with these financial

Systemic Risks

concepts were likely frustrated with my simplified butchering of them, and those unfamiliar with finance probably got lost in trying to follow along. Therein lies the junction of these two worlds. Entire populations have access to play with extremely sophisticated financial instruments, with no knowledge of or interest in how they work and are designed by experts who would be unable to explain it to them even if they tried.

Tom Hearden, a manager and senior trader at Skylands Capital, found an easy way to explain what XIV is: "The products in question are a derivative of a derivative of a derivative." Next chapter we explore how a WallStreetBets user added one more layer to these volatility derivatives to earn himself the all-time most valuable player (MVP) status for gambling on WallStreetBets.

8. WallStreetBets Most Valuable Player

The greatest design feature to have been built into the internet, coded deep into the software, was the ability to produce an endless supply of innovators who constantly find ways to surprise the unsurprisable. Even the most seasoned veterans who have seen it all can expect to be surprised on a regular basis.

SUPERM4N is one such innovator. He earned all sorts of accolades on WSB: He was the first user to discover a variant of the free money cheat code (almost a year before the heavily publicized ShapeTheMessaging episode), he single-handedly got his broker to ban a certain type of options trade called *box spreads* for everyone, he was responsible for setting the worldwide record on Google Trends for the search term "box spreads" in over a decade, he received an honorable mention on Wikipedia's "Box Spread (Options)" article, and he was the first WSB trader to end up with a negative balance in his brokerage

WallStreetBets Most Valuable Player

account,[16] after managing to withdraw 100 percent profit from his trade before things blew up.

Most importantly, he somehow managed to combine all the elements that have been discussed in this book in a single trade. He is a rookie trader who got himself into options trades he didn't understand. Using leveraged VIX ETFs and cheat codes, he exploited the asymmetric risk relationship between him, his broker, and the exchange, and he documented the entire journey publicly on WallStreetBets.

On Friday January 11, 2019, SUPERM4N made a post to WSB with the title "I don't know when to stop..." and he tagged it under the category YOLO. The post linked to a screenshot from his phone, which summarized his trade. As usual, the screenshot was difficult to interpret and required some explanation by the curious readers of WSB. It showed he had an open position with two thousand options contracts of UVXY, a leveraged VIX ETF worth nearly $300,000.

What SUPERM4N did was to trade options combinations known as box spreads. These are complicated options arbitrage strategies, which by definition are supposed to be risk free when implemented correctly. They're *delta neutral,* meaning they are bets that are indifferent as to the direction in which UVXY moves. Instead, they rely on making profit from pricing

---

[16] There is an example of a user who managed to get a negative $10,000 bank account balance by attempting a "cheat code" akin to overdrawing his checking account.

inefficiencies. In other words, they're simultaneous bets, which are both bought and sold, that the price will both go up and down. They're also not very common because, prior to commission-free brokers, trading these box spreads required buying and selling so many options that commissions would typically eat away most of the profit opportunity from trading them. After SUPERM4N posted his trade on WallStreetBets, Google Trends set a new worldwide record for the search term dating back to 2008.

SUPERM4N started his trade with around $5,000 in his account, and his initial trade only included eight of these box spreads. Usually, assigning a dollar value to a trade or bet is straightforward: simply add up the money spent on buying the options (and commissions if applicable). But when it comes to these types of trades, which include both buying and selling

WallStreetBets Most Valuable Player

options, the math becomes trickier since money is added and subtracted to the account as part of the same trade. SUPERM4N's broker, which had started offering options trading only a few months prior, likely learned of these intricacies the hard way.

Box Spreads at an all time high. Nobody know what they are. (i.redd.it)
submitted 11 months ago by Xehq to r/wallstreetbets
88 comments

[-] reddicure 229 points 11 months ago
That first spike on Jan 10 is from the RH brokers trying to figure out what the fuck he did

Rather than holding the necessary collateral for the original eight box spreads open in SUPERM4N's $5,000 account, his broker simply added and subtracted the money for each box spread—which in his case meant he ended up with more money after each bet he opened. Typically, brokers handle these trades by crediting traders' accounts with the extra money but not allowing them to use the extra money until the trades are closed to protect themselves and customers against something called *assignment risk*. When SUPERM4N noticed this oversight from his broker, he decided to repeat the same trade over and over until the market closed.

[-] **SUPERM4N** [S] 211 points 12 months ago

I started the position with 8 call spreads for a credit of 4.95 each about a week and a half ago, so my initial investment was 40 dollars. I legged in lots of 5 to begin with, then 20, 30, 50 alternating on each side. This all happened today, I would've kept going, but market closes at 4..

After all, the trade was meant to be an arbitrage opportunity that was supposed to be risk free. He figured—why not go all in? By the time he was done, SUPERM4N's total bet was a massive $287,000 position using options on leveraged VIX ETFs that were trading for around $70 at the time. Remember, options themselves are leveraged at one hundred-to-one and each box spread required a total of four options. Here's the math on what his account was controlling:

$$\frac{\begin{array}{c}(500 \text{ box spreads})\\(4 \text{ contracts each})\\(\$70 \text{ per UVXY share})\\\times (100 \text{ shares per contract})\end{array}}{\$14,000,000}$$

But SUPERM4N was not worried. In his eyes, there was literally no way he could lose money.

[-] SUPERM4N [S] 490 points 12 months ago 🏆 2 ⑤
It's credit spreads so I got paid when I opened it. It literally
cannot go tits up, max loss is 500 per spread but I got paid
594.

The post got a lot of attention and quickly became the top post on WallStreetBets. Lots of people chimed in, both experienced and novice, everyone with a different opinion. One of the forum moderators, a self-proclaimed options expert who goes by the name CHAINSAW_VASECTOMY, felt the need to make a disclaimer comment and permanently pin it to the top of the thread. He also *distinguished* his comment, which is a special power WSB moderators have that make their remarks more prominent and is usually used when officially speaking on behalf of the subreddit itself as opposed to just sharing personal opinions. This type of distinguished comment is used sparingly, as moderators usually give WSB users wide latitude to do as they please. But the risk for misinformation was so big, he felt the moral obligation to intervene.

[-] CHAINSAW_VASECTOMY [M] 1554 points 12 months ago* - stickied comment
DO NOT DO THIS. OP has an account of 5k but due to robinhood
shitty margining he has 200K of risk on due to early exercise.

In the end his instincts were right. *Early exercise* in this case is the same as the *assignment* risk referenced earlier. I won't get into details of what this means, but I'll add that this risk was ironically responsible for flipper321 making $110,000 by accident. Sure enough, SUPERM4N got assigned a bunch of options, and his perfect trade started to unravel.

[–] SUPERM4N [S] 4511 points 12 months ago
Ok, so I got assigned on 283 of the 10 strike calls. I mistakenly underestimated assignment risk due to the underlying having no dividends. At this point I am still net positive on this trade but will be scaling out ASAP. BTW Robinhood closed my account and is trying to close my position, even though I'm not in a margin call.

However, before his trade started to really go against him, he apparently managed to withdraw $10,000 from his account, taking the whole concept of risk asymmetry to a new level—he was able to take out profits while his broker was left holding the tremendous risk from a losing trade.

[–] SUPERM4N [S] 413 points 12 months ago
Not if I can scale out of the remaining position at favorable prices... I withdrew 10k yesterday which is twice my original account value and I'm not in a margin call, But that could easily change.

A few days later, SUPERM4N made a new post with an update titled "Only invest what you can afford to lose they said..." and linked to another screenshot of his cell phone's broker account, which showed a negative balance of nearly $60,000 and a notice that his account had been closed.

WallStreetBets Most Valuable Player

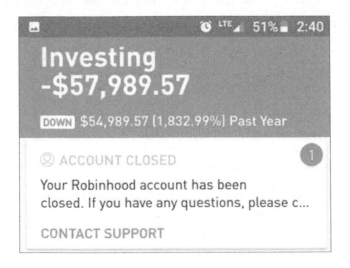

From the comments:

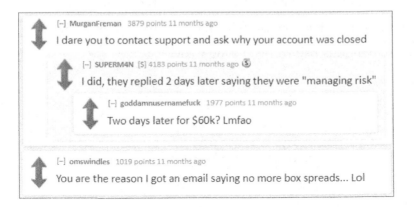

Indeed, his broker promptly changed its company-wide policy and made the decision to prevent customers from trading box spreads altogether. The email that was sent to every customer read:

Subject: Important Information about Box Spreads

We're reaching out to you to let you know that we're no longer supporting box spreads on Robinhood.

A box spread is an options strategy created by opening a call spread and put spread with the same strike prices and expiration dates. Box spreads are often mistaken for an arbitrage opportunity; however, they have hidden risks that could lead to losing much more money than expected. These significant risks have led us to remove the ability to trade box spreads from our platform.

At this time, you won't be able to open new box spread positions. If you currently own a box spread, we may close that position. We apologize for any inconvenience and hope you understand that we've made this decision with you in mind.

You can learn more about box spreads by visiting our Help Center. Please reach out if you have any questions.

SUPERM4N's episode was so spectacular that it drew the attention of the media as well.

WallStreetBets Most Valuable Player

The headline is technically inaccurate. SUPERM4N made and successfully withdrew $5,000 (in addition to his original $5,000 deposit). A more accurate headline would have read "Trader says he has 'none of *his own* money at risk,' then promptly loses almost 2,000% of his broker's money."

9. Spotlight

Google   "wallstreetbets"

A Robinhood Exploit Let Redditors Bet Infinite Money on the ...
VICE - Nov 6, 2019
Redditors in the irony-poisoned Wall Street Bets (r/**wallstreetbets**) community
discovered an exploit in the investing app Robinhood they've ...

'If I had made the right trade I would have been retired now ...
Business Insider - Nov 23, 2019
Tomatotowers, who learned about the bug on the **WallStreetBets** subreddit, took out
$300,000 worth of leverage with a $5,000 deposit.

How one investor's Amazon misfire led to a 99% loss in his ...
MarketWatch - Dec 11, 2018
If you're feeling bruised and battered by this whipsaw stock market, you might
consider heading over to Reddit's "**WallStreetBets**" board.

Facebook's Drop Just Cost 24-Year-Old Options Trader ...
Barron's - Jul 26, 2018
Rather than slither away into the internet ether, Cao took his medicine on Reddit's
"**WallStreetBets**" forum, where he first announced his ...

The media plays an important role in all of this as well. Its frequent cheerleader-style coverage of the shenanigans found on WSB is akin to crowds that gather around bullies at schoolyard fights. They "oohh" and "aahh" while filming with their cell phones, hoping to catch a good clip to upload to get lots of *likes* on social media.

Who could blame them? What happens at WallStreetBets is exciting, but the media's attraction to this genre of stories is nothing new. In fact, the media has a long history of covering and selling gambling when it comes to lottery tickets. Big wins and losses are exhilarating for any spectator; they drive traffic and it makes perfect sense to cover them. It's the American dream—even though playing the seemingly innocuous lottery is statistically worse than games at a casino if one considers the odds of winning. News outlets nationwide dedicate stories that build up big upcoming Powerball jackpots and then follow up with touching stories about the winners. They do the same with

WSB. Matt Levine from Bloomberg referred to flipper321's $110,000 accidental win as "a heartwarming story from r/wallstreetbets." It's no surprise that journalists from serious financial outlets follow the official @wallstreetbets Twitter account to keep up with the latest news coming out of the subreddit.

It's a predicament, however, as the media's involvement inevitably encourages people to engage in the very risky behavior they cover. It's hard to ignore how inspirational stories romanticizing traders' tales of turning $1,000 into $100,000 can lure others to try to follow suit. The same could be said for people simply looking to perform outlandish stunts just to get attention.

This is a long-standing ethical and philosophical dilemma for journalism. The topic comes up in a more tragic light whenever there is a school shooting and news organizations are faced with the difficult balancing act of covering the events while trying not to put a spotlight on the shooter, which has often been found to be a motive for that sort of crime.

It's impossible to tell for sure whether the media has a direct causal effect between their coverage of stories and subsequent copycats encouraged by the attention, but nonetheless they've unanimously taken steps toward addressing the problem. Many, if not most outlets refuse to name the shooter and instead choose to focus on the victims instead.

But few debates exist around the coverage of uplifting stories

Spotlight

like lottery winners and whether publicity surrounding it inherently tempts people to participate in it. Without knowing it, the media could be responsible for propagating its own form of peer pressure with its own catchy acronym—FOMO—for Fear of Missing Out. All the while, stories seldom focus on the millions of people who lost money trying to win.

In the end, whether the media encourages the types of gambling behaviors displayed on WSB or not, the attention is clearly welcomed.

10. The Future

The future of trading and Wall Street in general should be interesting. The brokerage industry is changing at such a fast pace that between the completion of this book and when the editing process was finished, Charles Schwab acquired TD Ameritrade, Robinhood launched the ability to purchase fractional shares, and Vanguard—arguably the Holy Grail of safe investing—which is known for low commission index funds, is now offering stock options commission free. In June of 2019, the SEC officially approved "nontransparent" ETFs, which allow their issuers to disclose their holdings a few times a year instead of daily. Cryptocurrencies are well on their way to becoming indoctrinated with Wall Street's seal of approval, since Bitcoin futures started trading on the Chicago Mercantile Exchange in 2017. And it won't be long before cryptocurrency ETFs, which will undoubtedly be accompanied by stock options, are approved. It's impossible to predict what the landscape will

The Future

look like once this cycle of disruption takes shape.

With all these changes, there is one important topic that, although it seldom comes up on WallStreetBets, deserves some attention: automation.

Millennials and members of Generation Z (referred to sometimes as *Zoomers*) are tech savvy. They've grown up with a smartphone in one hand and a battery charger in the other. It's common to find people from these generations who have taught themselves computer programming from the endless selection of free online resources. It's only a matter of time before a niche group decides to combine automated programming with gambling.

Algorithmic trading communities already exist, but they're mostly serious and can be compared to the serious investing-style communities that existed prior to WallStreetBets. This is likely because anyone wanting to get involved with algorithmic trading today will face similar high barriers of entry comparable to those faced by amateurs who were interested in trading ten years ago. Platforms that support automated trading are scarce and expensive, and opening accounts with them are often more tedious than the gamified Candy Crush app experience. At some point in the not too distant future, it's logical that brokers looking for a competitive edge will offer easy-to-use automated trading features to set themselves apart.

Alpaca nabs $6M for stocks API so anyone can build a Robinhood

Josh Constine @joshconstine / 1:06 pm CST · November 8, 2019   ☐ Comment

In November 2019, Alpaca Securities LLC secured series A funding for $6 million. The company, whose slogan is literally "Hack Financial Systems," aims to let users build automated systems and trade with real-time market data for free. And they're not restricting themselves to the US market. They want to let everybody make their own automated version of Robinhood, anywhere in the world. Alpaca acts simultaneously as a broker that allows commission-free trading, short selling, high frequency trading, and margin accounts and as an Application Programming Interface (API)—a sort of plug and play for programmers to easily automate their strategies. Although the company is still in its infant stages, its ambitious goals are likely to further send shockwaves through an already turbulent marketplace.

Business Wire
A Berkshire Hathaway Company

"Alpaca is on track to become a much-needed solution for the growing number of algorithmic investing enthusiasts who may require a commission-free brokerage to automate their investing," said Jared Broad, founder and CEO of QuantConnect.

The Future

Everything about the phrase "Automated investing enthusiast" is an oxymoron. Yet it's the choice of words used by Jared Broad, founder and CEO of QuantConnect, when describing Alpaca's potential. Serious investors are not enthusiasts. And anyone familiar with the tremendous complexities involved with algorithmic trading knows automation belongs nowhere near amateur investors. Even for WSB's risk appetite, automation is too much. A recent post by someone looking for feedback on an algorithm he had developed was met with heavy resistance.

[–] 1st_Amendment_EndRun 10 points 🏅

Based on some things I've seen in machine learning implementations, there's no way in fuck I'm going to expose my money to some random amateur's fiddle fucking around in anaconda so they can learn all the things that can go wrong.

Further, Renaissance (please check your spelling checker) Technologies has a small army of industry professionals (in addition to the mathematicians, physicists and other weirdos they employ) that keep a close eye on anything they have that's automated.

Algorithms have already been known to cause problems in the market. In late 2012, a trading glitch in Knight Capital Group, which accidentally bought stocks it wasn't supposed to, caused it to lose $10 million per minute—$440 million by the time the company turned the rogue computer off.

In May 2010, the Dow Jones lost nearly 9 percent in what was called a flash crash and largely blamed on high frequency trading. In fact, much of the events of that day were blamed on a single rogue trader named Navinder Singh Sarao, who lived with his parents at the time and used an algorithm that faked orders to manipulate market prices. Although he was arrested and the practice of *spoofing orders* is now banned, the conditions that fostered his behavior are well intact. At the time, he had found and exploited a sophisticated loophole which allowed him to make millions of dollars. The inadvertent externality was temporarily erasing nearly $1 trillion of value from the stock market.

These flash crashes are intertwined with the complexities of other moving parts like ETFs. In August 2015, another flash crash resulted in a 5 percent decline in the S&P 500. This was further exacerbated by delays and circuit breakers meant to protect the stock market from collapsing. Controls are put in place to shut down specific stock trading when their prices fall too fast—but this created complications for the futures and ETFs that tracked those stocks and couldn't establish their fair value. This led traders to continue selling and adding to the falling market prices. Remember, ETFs were designed to track prices of other things, not the other way around.

Increasingly the financial system is becoming more globalized, complex, interconnected, interdependent, correlated, and full of mechanisms that affect it in unpredictable ways. News of Brexit affects Microsoft's market value. Drunken traders in London push up prices for oil futures around the globe. Even tweets from a hacked Associated Press account or from an angry

The Future

Donald Trump can violently swing major indices in seconds. A single trader with a $2,000 account cannot affect the structural integrity of the market. But the prospect of allowing millions of ambitious amateurs with a proven record of finding and abusing weaknesses to plug their high frequency experiments into the global financial system should have regulators worried.

Post Flash Crash, Regulators Still Use Bicycles To Catch Ferraris

11. Conclusion

The stock market has a long and important history. It grew from a necessity for growing companies to raise capital, with the first recorded transaction dating back to the early 1600s when the Dutch East India Company issued the first paper shares. Shortly after, the idea spread around the world and became a prominent force that fueled the industrial revolution and modern manufacturing. It played a pivotal role in propelling America during the nineteenth century into being a global superpower. Wall Street is a symbol of American capitalism.

Today, even though the fundamental system behind the stock market has not changed, the role of it has. It is more common for companies to raise private capital during their growth stage and then take the company public afterward, once they're valuable enough, to compensate investors and founders with the money raised from the IPO.

The way stock exchanges operate has changed as well.

Computers have all but replaced iconic floor traders and brokers, commonly depicted in movies holding up pieces of paper while shouting at each other in a seemingly senseless manner. Getting access to trade on the floor was (and still is) a very selective process, requiring participants to have significant capital, knowledge, and experience before being considered. This also served as a barrier to entry for ordinary people who were interested in trading stocks, which meant nonprofessionals were forced to hire brokers who had individuals on the exchange floor. But now these floor traders are computers, and it has become relatively easy for brokers to buy virtual seats at stock exchanges, which in turn has exploded the number of available brokers. The structure of trading has changed as well. Lots of these zero-commission brokers don't even buy and sell stocks on the official stock exchange, instead they allow third parties known as *dark pools* to do it themselves.

What was once a system for raising money to grow a business is now an arbitrary high-tech system of fluctuating numbers. It is estimated by the World Bank that the global market capitalization (size of all publicly traded companies) is $69 trillion. The derivatives market, however, is an astounding $1.2 quadrillion. To put that into perspective, for every one dollar of value that exists in a share of a given company (the kind you can explain to a five-year-old), seventeen dollars exist in the acronym-laden, leveraged, counterparty dependent, and abstract variety that WSB uses for YOLO bets.

SUPPLY AND DEMAND

WallStreetBets started because no community existed online that welcomed people looking for aggressive investing strategies that weren't afraid of high risks and high rewards. As the years went on, WSB evolved into something I never would have imagined—an all-out casino.

Reddit is among the best examples of new age democracies; its entire structure is founded on a voting system. Posts and comments are ranked by popularity, communities are run by volunteers, and everybody has a voice. Perhaps the evolution of WSB can be explained with Economics 101 logic: I supplied a space for trading, but the community demanded a place to gamble.

Andrew Stewart of Exchange Capital Management was quoted in *Forbes*, saying:

> Certainly, commission-free trading makes it easier for reckless traders to ruin themselves even faster with fewer speedbumps. Using that as an argument against lowering the cost of trading, though, is a bit like complaining that your family's unlimited data plan is to blame for the kids using their phones at the dinner table.

Andrew is right. It takes more than just commission-free

Conclusion

brokers to embolden millions of people to actively participate in the kind of reckless behavior shown on WSB. Creating such a massive trend requires a convergence between a creative generation left wounded from a financial crisis, the opportunity provided by a proliferation of brokers along with complacent regulation, and an endless supply of high-risk tools that are increasingly available to the public. Of course, some people are probably just attracted to the thrill of making and losing money like they do in Las Vegas.

A consistent theme observed on WallStreetBets is millennials trying to get out of a rat race. They're motivated to make reckless trades in hopes to win big lump sums to then invest responsibly. They're quite creative, collaborative, and fearless in their efforts to achieve their goals. They've also taken a page out of the too-big-to-fail banking playbook and figured out how to outsource their risk for personal gain (in most cases legally).

The brokerage industry is faced with its own supply and demand equation as well. It found a new business model with perverse incentives—a model that values volume over risk. Despite all the high-risk traders who are happy to let others carry the *assignment* risks associated with options, brokers are still flocking to them. This model is so successful that even old-school brokers that were traditionally associated with pushing low-risk index funds were forced to join others in offering commission-free stock options to avoid the fear of missing out. There's no closing this Pandora's box.

Reporting by major news outlets also poses a moral hazard. Consumers of outlandish gambling stories are clearly entertained and offer profitable incentives to the media organizations who provide them, and coverage of this behavior reinforces it.

Meanwhile, the government and regulative bodies in charge of overseeing these activities are providing little help as their policies are outdated and often contradicting.

WHO CAN FIX IT?

There's clear concern with the pace at which the number of traders with no discernable personal-risk tolerance are joining Wall Street, coupled with the number of brokers willing to give them unrestricted access. This demographic has an unfathomable comfort with taking chances. They're breaking current risk models, which rely on common sense and self-preservation. Brokers' approach of trying to stop them by plugging holes, like blocking box spreads or *deep in the money (DITM) covered calls*,[17] is like trying to save a sinking ship by dumping out water using buckets.

Some suggest imposing tougher access controls, by means of even harder questionnaires when opening new accounts, would limit people accessing high-risk tools. The idea being only people with a certain level of knowledge should be allowed to trade

---

[17] DITM covered calls is the more specific name for the covered calls used in the free money cheat code.

Conclusion

131

dangerous securities. There are multiple problems with this approach.

First, not all the high-risk trades that take place on WSB require high-risk access levels. For example, covered calls (the ones used for the free money cheat code) are the safest maneuver there is in the world of options. They're used by the most conservative investors and are even welcomed on risk-averse communities like r/investing. They are the equivalent of owning stock and listing them at an auction for sale at a higher price. In fact, they're so safe they're allowed to be traded on the lowest options risk level accounts.

Second, most of the users on WSB are quite sophisticated and would pass most tests with flying colors. It's how they successfully look for and find exploits in the first place. For example, one of the guys who leveraged $4,000 into $1 million during the free money cheat code frenzy was asked why he chose Ford as a company to sell covered calls:

[-] milkcarton232   42 points 2 months ago

Why Ford?

> [-] high_on_ford [S] 252 points 2 months ago ✓
>
> Good question, basically comes down to three things.
> * Cheap, you can start the chain with $850. My account value was ~4k but my cash position was only like $1600 when I started.
> * There's a ton of liquidity on Ford, getting filled by an MM on the ITM calls was easy and could basically be done at intrinsic value
> * Its not very volatile, which is helpful when the position is only being used to generate leverage and not to actually create any profit. The fact that it went up $.50 while I was holding it surprised me.
>
> Also I just really like Ford as a stock, have some in my Roth that I sell covered calls against.

His answer took me by surprise. It showed he had total clarity over what he was doing and a complete understanding behind the mechanics of this cheat code.

His answer also provided some interesting insight into how he uses the market—on one hand, he has a $4,000 Robinhood account to leverage $1 million for a high-profile and very high-risk YOLO trade, and on the other hand, he sells covered calls against his Ford investment in his Roth IRA. The two strategies could not be further from each other.

How can you convince someone to take the market seriously or to reduce risk when they already take it seriously and already use the lowest-risk investment strategies imaginable? High_on_ford obviously understands advanced market concepts and has a responsible retirement fund yet keeps a funded broker app for high risk YOLO bets for kicks.

Conclusion

Brokers could also increase minimum account balance requirements to filter out some of the amateurs, but it's a double-edged sword. Irresponsible traders that make it through the filter would be equipped to inflict a lot more damage. Besides, all tendencies are pointing toward the opposite direction with no account minimums, zero commissions, and fractional shares. Their incentives are incompatible with this approach altogether. Their aim is to get the greatest number of customers, not fewer.

Regulators could try to step in, but they have their own set of unique challenges. They are historically slow due to their bureaucratic structure and are working in an environment that is experiencing incredibly fast change. The government is reactive by nature, which means it would likely close loopholes once they've already been exposed instead of proactively preventing them. Additional challenges revolve around creating rules or laws that don't adversely affect serious funds. Gamblers and investors alike are playing in the same field, and any regulatory changes would have to be very carefully designed to avoid harming those in the latter category. Even if they succeeded in making effective regulatory changes in the US, the financial sector is becoming increasingly globalized by the day. Robinhood is launching in the United Kingdom soon, and it's unlikely to be their final stop. The tight, interconnected nature of financial systems makes restrictions in only one part of the world pointless. It would require a coordinated, collaborative worldwide effort to implement any meaningful reforms.

CASINO ON WALL STREET

Serious onlookers might feel indignation by what happens on WSB, but millennials are simply treating Wall Street for what it is—a huge casino made for them to play in. A legal venue full of leveraged tools to make sophisticated bets with from their cell phones. There's nothing new about this concept; there have been plenty of serious commentators who have drawn comparisons between Wall Street and casinos. What's new is that millennials are celebrating and acting on this idea instead of shunning it. They're finding entertaining ways to hopefully make big money on a very public stage. Spectators also enjoy watching what happens on WallStreetBets because of the refreshing sense of honesty displayed that doesn't exist anywhere else.

These millennials are playing with fancy toys, some of which they profess not to understand or even care to understand. I could make the argument that even some brokers don't fully understand them either. These toys were designed by Wall Street, delivered to them by industry insiders, and then sanctioned by the government. David Faber warned on his CNBC show with Jim Cramer, "Every single time we have a crisis, we realize all the things Wall Street has created that come back to haunt us."

When the next financial crisis comes, and it will come, I suspect that media coverage and public sentiment regarding WallStreetBets will sour. What's fun and heartwarming now will

Conclusion

135

quickly turn to outrage and disgust as the public will need a place to channel their anger, and WSB will be an easy scapegoat. It's easier to point the finger at a group of rebellious traders than an entire system.

Today we have youngsters trading during their lunch breaks from their cell phones, placing $1 million bets, which they don't have. They're waking up surprised, with over $20 million worth of shares, which they didn't mean to buy, using borrowed money, which they didn't mean to borrow, in their accounts. Traders who deposit several thousand dollars somehow end up owing six figures to their brokers, with no chance of ever paying it back. And they're playing in the same arena as the trained professionals—who work behind actual Bloomberg terminals—at Goldman Sachs. Morgan Stanley may have big account balances, but millennials know how to get infinite leverage using cheat codes, and they come in droves. They're collectively behind the wheel of millions of accounts that aren't equipped with safety switches, and brokers want to get even more of them. Because like in casinos—it's all just a number's game.

* * *

As for what happened with World_Chaos, the high schooler who turned $900 into $55,000 four years ago? After going off to college and disappearing from the spotlight, he recently resurfaced. He made a post on WallStreetBets depicting a trading account with over a quarter of $1 million and said, "Now that I'm about to graduate I'm more free to yolo."

Many of you know me as the 900 to 55k guy, I've been missing since I went to college. Now that I'm about to graduate I'm more free to yolo.
submitted 8 months ago to r/wallstreetbets
261 comments

I actually spoke with him recently, and the truth turned out to be even more interesting. Before going to college, World_Chaos took the money from his wins and invested it into a passive and carefully selected portfolio. He was able to successfully grow his earnings in a relatively safe manner (relative to WSB, that is). He has no intention of gambling his money away; in fact he chose to get into real estate after using some of that money as a down payment for a condo in New York. World_Chaos is yet another example of a big WallStreetBets winner who chose to take the money from his high-risk payout and responsibly invest it into his future. He understands perfectly well the risks involved with the trades that frequent WSB, and he too decided to go the safe route after scoring big on a YOLO.

Conclusion

12.   Best of WSB

Below is a sample of some thought provoking and some humorous posts made on WallStreetBets throughout the years. In some cases, I included some of the top replies from the comments.

Can we fight a recession by pretending it doesn't exist?

Posting from an alt because this might be a nuclear tier stupid question but if we just invest like normal then how can there be a recession? And if we don't invest like normal, aren't we helping to create the recession?

Thanks
—Optimisticmoney

Guys I just had an idea for a new trading app

It's like Tinder but for options. Each FD shows stats, pictures of the CEO, and news articles and if you swipe right you instantly buy that option. Also once a day you get one free super like and each option shows how many people have super-liked it. What do you all think, potential Robinhood killer?

—Samrockswin

Everything is priced in

Don't even ask the question. The answer is yes, it's priced in. Think Amazon will beat the next earnings? That's already been priced in. You work at the drive thru for Mickey D's and found out that the burgers are made of human meat? Priced in. You think insiders don't already know that? The market is an all powerful, all encompassing being that knows the very inner workings of your subconscious before you were even born. Your very existence was priced in decades ago when the market was valuing Standard Oil's expected future earnings based on population growth that would lead to your birth, what age you would get a car, how many times you would drive your car every week, how many times you take the bus/train, etc. Anything you can think of has already been priced in, even the things you aren't thinking of. You have no original thoughts. Your consciousness is just an illusion, a product of the omniscient market. Free will is a myth. The market sees all, knows all and will be there from the beginning of time until the end of the universe (the market has already priced in the heat death of the universe). So please, before you make a post on wsb asking whether AAPL has priced in earpods 11 sales or whatever, know that it has already been priced in and don't ask such a dumb fucking question again.

—zsd99

From the comments:

But is the pricing in priced in tho?

—theknowndude

Why don't economists pick up $100 dollar bills off the street? If it was worth it, someone would have grabbed it already.

—Kule7

Efficient markets cannot exist

Note this is from the same author as the previous post:

The efficient market hypothesis assumes that you cannot beat the market because investors are rational, thus, assets are priced accurately because of this rationality. However, the existence of WSB disproves this. Taking the example of the WSB user that bought $50k of LULU calls and proceeded to lose it all, in an efficient market, this trade shouldn't exist as it is literally free money for the opposing trader.

Therefore, I conclude efficient markets do not exist.

—zsd99

Why is it so much easier to lose money than to make money?

Legit. If I want to tank 50% of my account balance I can do it in 15 minutes. If I want to grow 3% it takes 3 weeks. It's incredible. what are the reasons for this? Talking about going short and long here.

—BadGeorge

The question itself is a wonderful philosophical question but the answers were even more thought provoking. The most upvoted comment was from appropriately named user Theocletian, who thought it best to use the laws of thermodynamics to explain:

Believe it or not, the general idea that it is easier to lose money than to gain money in a closed system mirrors the law of entropy.

This is to say that the ability to gain and maintain monetary funds is behaviorally entropic because:

1. Money is an arbitrary construct that is determined by a

collective belief it itself.

2. Due to the nature of the need to acquire money, there is a dynamic such that it is far more common to desire to make money rather than to lose it.

It is similar to how a molecule behaves in that it desires a low energy state (i.e. a resting state) and will only accept a high energy state if forced into it or there are other circumstances such that it is made to react with something else.

Humans naturally rest in the "losing/spending money" state because it is by far the lower energy state of the two. It is "easy" and people can do it naturally without much difficulty. Further, groups of people behave similar to chemical macrostates and tend to assist each other in their ability to lose money.

The chaos associated with the closed system is such that it must always increase, and in the stock market this is no exception. In order for you to win, someone else has to lose. It is much easier to lose because it takes a lot more resources to create order in your part of the system when it wants to tend towards disorder.

This is also why you naturally feel somewhat uneasy after a big win. We all understand the Gambler's Fallacy, yet cannot shake the feeling that we are going to lose it all on the next set of plays even after a major win. This is again due to the notion that you cannot be expected to maintain such a high energy state for an extended period of time without some extraneous circumstances bolstering you.

Irreversibility is another important factor on the topic of entropy because it effectively gives the system a direction in which to tend. For example, if you bought a regretful purchase, you may be able to return it at the store with minimal effort. However, you cannot waive away the losses from a shitty spread. The more irreversible a system is, the more likely it will be difficult to create order in such a system because it always wants to go in one direction.

The other part of the issue is just pure psychology. It is far easier to note the thousands of steps left ahead of you rather than the millions that you have already taken. Minor wins are quickly forgotten whereas even small losses are often the focus of mental anguish. People often place too much importance on wins, whether it is the sheer amount and/or the frequency to understand that what is far more important is how they lose. Learning to lose well is a life skill that is incredibly underrated because everyone is fucking obsessed with winning everything every time everywhere.

— Theocletian

A brief history of the YOLO

1. Jessie Livermore becomes the first true YOLOer, with a string of hugely successful yolo's. Shorts the 1929 crash.

Best of WSB

Makes over a billion in todays money on his big short. His edge? He practically invented technical analysis. Ultimately loses it all, because that is just how he rolled, mother fucker. Key quote: "Play the market only when all factors are in your favor. No person can play the market all the time and win."

2. George Soros Starts an incredibly successful hedge fund. Bets against the bank of England in '92. Makes over a billion dollars on his big short. His edge? He hired someone smarter than him (Druckenmiller), and then encouraged the guy to go for the jugular when his animal instincts said there was a sure kill. Key quote: "There is no point in being confident and having a small position."

3. John Paulson Starts a very successful hedge fund. Shorts the housing market in '08. Makes over 3 billion dollars for himself, 15 billion total, on his big short. His edge? He hired someone smarter than him (Pellegrini) and went balls to the wall with other peoples money when it seemed like they were on to something. Key quote: "We found the El Dorado of investments. Are we going to just dip our toes in?"

To summarize, I would like to quote the god father of the YOLOr, Jesse Livermore one more time.

"The game of speculation is the most uniformly fascinating game in the world. But it is not a game for the stupid, the mentally lazy, the person of inferior emotional balance, or the get-rich-quick adventurer. They will die poor."
—whythedownboats

Top comment:

4. Nelson Bunker Hunt, an oilman, who attempted to corner the worlds silver market in the 70s. Ended up holding a third of the global supply, caused silver to go from $11 an ounce to over 50 and profited close to 4 billion. Got dick slapped by the government and lost it all. His edge? Massive fucking balls.

Key qoute: "To be successful, you must decide exactly what you want to accomplish, then resolve to pay the price to get it."

—natwwal23

Bunch of p******

Alright! Listen up you a***** fucks, there has been a recent influx of people being concern if "it's the right time to invest" or "everything is so overvalued". So what? You know how I see this shit. The stock market is like Yellowstone, like ya that bitch is going to blow up but is that going to stop me from creating a booking to Yellowstone hotel, grabbing as much blow and hookers as I can on the way. Fuck no, i plan on waking up every morning watching ole faithful blow from my bedroom. Conveniently, that's also the name of the 80 year old hooker that I brought. I'm going to die no matter what might as well bring a few accounts with me along the way. Oh, and finally PERMABULL WILL NEVER END.

—GWithL

The first one is free

Why is it that when we got into options, we all made money on our first measly call buy but then proceed to lose money after that? I'll tell you why, the first one is always free. I have a plan to not only make everyone in this sub money, but establish wsb as the ruling party of the world. Here's the plan.

Step 1: everyone close out of your positions, your probably going to lose all your money anyways.

Step 2: Find some idiot that has zero knowledge of options. Have him open a Robinhood account with option trading. Tell him that if he buys a call and the stock goes up, you make money, buy a put and the stock goes down, you make money.

Step 3: Have everyone wire the idiot their money.

Step 4: Have him go all in on one position, buying as many contracts as possible.

Step 5: Watch as we get 400% roi

Step 6: Take that money and find a new idiot; go back to step 2.

Complete the cycle a couple times, establish world domination. Thank me later r******

—The_Pandemonium

Fractional Shares [gonna] kill the economy bros

Okay... commission free? Whatever, now I can put that money into more tendies. But partial goddamn shares has got to be the most a******* thing ever. If you don't have enough money to buy a single share of something then you legit just can't afford that shit and that's okay.

Fucking Acorns, Stash, Robinhood, and the goddamn Ca$hApP trying to make the stock market into something everyone should be throwing their money into when it's the last place a poor person should be stashing their money.

Seriously, yeah it doesn't seem like a big deal at first glance that some dude at McDanks is putting $5 a check into Tesla or AAPL because they're fuckin dope... but bruh there is soooooo many poor people out there afraid of losing their money in the market because it seems like all you hear about is people losing their shirts or becoming millionaires. Now every dude with $20 and a Robinhood account is gonna think he's hot shit and the second we have a downturn 200,000,000 new a******* are gonna panic sell their $47 in Tesla.

I'm not completely r*******, I'm sure there's something in there that the broker owns the underlying asset or something and there is precautions in place but I think we all know what happened the last time a bunch of fucks who couldn't afford the shit they were buying jumped head first into that shit. (come on, 2008 ya shits.)

Idk, maybe my tinfoil hat is a little tight but I don't like this shit at all bros.

—theoddman92

I need something safe-ish to hold, potentially through a recession. How do things like bond ETF's perform?

I have a certain piece of my portfolio that I need to hold and not lose for the next 6-12 months. It's from a loan I had to take out for other reasons, with 7% interest. I'd like to mitigate part of the interest while I have the money. What's a kinda safe thing I can put it in? I'm kinda looking for a low-risk 3-5% that's not going to implode during a recession.

—TheSkyPirate

Safest thing to hold is your dick as I am sure it never sees any action

—BallsofSt33l

REFERENCES

(n.d.). Retrieved from https://subredditstats.com/

2090. Know Your Customer. (n.d.). Retrieved from Financial Industry Regulatory Authority: https://www.finra.org/rules-guidance/rulebooks/finra-rules/2090

Baer, N., Barry, E., & Smith, G. (2019, May 4). *Economics Files.* Retrieved from POMONA College: http://economics-files.pomona.edu/GarySmith/Econ190/Econ190%202019/Baer,%20Barry%20Final%20Thesis%20vf.pdf

Bramble, Laura. (n.d.). How the Stock Market Was Started & by Whom. Small Business - Chron.com. Retrieved from http://smallbusiness.chron.com/stock-market-started-whom-14745.html

Byrne, B. (2016, May 22). *Reddit Thread Encourages Risky Millennial Traders To Make Insane Bets.* Retrieved from ValueWalk: https://www.valuewalk.com/2016/05/wallstreetbets-reddit/

Choi, J. (n.d.). *Homeownership and Living Arrangements among Millennials: New Sources of Wealth Inequality and What to Do about It.* Retrieved from New America: The Emerging Millennial Wealth Gap: https://www.newamerica.org/Millennials/reports/emerging-millennial-wealth-gap/homeownership-and-living-arrangements-among-Millennials-new-sources-of-wealth-inequality-and-what-to-do-about-it/

Chowdhry, A. (2019, December 5). *Robinhood now has over 10 million users.* Retrieved from Pulse 2.0: https://pulse2.com/robinhood-10-million-users/

Constine, J. (2019, November 8). *Alpaca nabs $6M for stocks API so anyone can build a Robinhood.* Retrieved from Tech Crunch: https://techcrunch.com/2019/11/08/alpaca-stock-trading-api/

Davidson, J. (2018, October 25). *Meet the Bros Behind /r/WallStreetBets, Who Lose Hundreds of Thousands of Dollars in a Day—And Brag About It.* Retrieved from money.com: https://money.com/wall-street-bets/

Dobbs, S. (2017, March 24). *7 of the Biggest Treasure Troves Ever Found.* Retrieved from Mental Floss: https://www.mentalfloss.com/article/90883/7-biggest-treasure-troves-ever-found

Evans, R. (2019, December 10). *ETFs That Hide Their Portfolios Get Go-Ahead From U.S. Regulator.* Retrieved from Bloomberg: Rachel Evans

Farrington, R. (2019, December 3). *Are Commission-Free Investing Apps Encouraging Reckless Behavior?* Retrieved from Forbes: https://www.forbes.com/sites/robertfarrington/2019/12/03/are-commission-free-investing-apps-encouraging-reckless-behavior/#43a8d61a2579

Farrington, R. (2019, December 30). *The Average Net Worth of Millennials by Age.* Retrieved from The College Investor: https://thecollegeinvestor.com/14611/average-net-worth-Millennials/

Feldman, A. (2011, April 16). *Sites changed with gambling offenses.* Retrieved from ESPN: http://www.espn.com/espn/poker/news/story?id=6362238

Financial Industry Regulatory Authority. (2019). *Financial Industry Regulatory Authority.* Retrieved from Day-Trading Margin

Best of WSB

Requirements: Know the Rules: https://www.finra.org/investors/learn-to-invest/advanced-investing/day-trading-margin-requirements-know-rules

Fuscaldo, D. (2019, December 4). *Mobile-Trading App Robinhood Now Has More Than 10 Million Accounts.* Retrieved from Forbes: https://www.forbes.com/sites/donnafuscaldo/2019/12/04/mobile-trading-app-robinhood-now-has-more-than-10-million-accounts/#6805e2903f81

Gurdus, L. (2019, October 2). *CNBC.* Retrieved from The SEC says it's making ETFs more accessible—here's what that could mean for investors: https://www.cnbc.com/2019/10/02/the-sec-says-its-making-etfs-more-accessiblewhat-that-could-mean.html

Gurdus, L. (2019, November 9). *ETF assets rise to record $4 trillion and top industry expert says it's still 'early days'.* Retrieved from CNBC: https://www.cnbc.com/2019/11/09/etf-assets-rise-to-a-record-4-trillion-and-its-still-early-days.html?__source=twitter%7Cmain

Gurdus, L. (2020, January 4). *Watch out for these ETF surprises in 2020, industry pros say* . Retrieved from CNBC: https://www.cnbc.com/amp/2020/01/03/watch-out-for-these-etf-surprises-in-2020-industry-pros-say.html

Hershey, W. (2019, July 22). *What is an ETF? The Ultimate Guide for Beginners.* Retrieved from Roundhill Investments: https://www.roundhillinvestments.com/blog/what-is-an-etf

Ingram, D. (2019, September 12). *Designed to Distract.* Retrieved from NBC News: https://www.nbcnews.com/tech/tech-news/confetti-push-notifications-stock-app-robinhood-nudges-investors-toward-risk-n1053071

Kiberd, R. (2017, December 11). *You Probably Shouldn't Bet Your Savings on Reddit's 'Wallstreetbets'.* Retrieved from Motherboard by Vice: https://www.vice.com/en_us/article/nedzqm/you-probably-shouldnt-bet-your-savings-on-reddits-wallstreetbets

Langlois, S. (2019, January 22). *Trader says he has 'no money at risk,' then promptly loses almost 2,000%.* Retrieved from MarketWatch: https://www.marketwatch.com/story/trader-says-he-has-no-money-at-risk-then-promptly-loses-almost-2000-2019-01-22

Langlois, S. F. (2016, April 5). *There's a loud corner of Reddit where Millennials look to get rich or die tryin'.* Retrieved from MarketWatch: https://www.marketwatch.com/story/the-Millennials-looking-to-get-rich-or-die-tryin-off-one-of-wall-streets-riskiest-oil-plays-2016-03-30

Levine, M. (2015, April 21). *Guy Trading at Home Caused the Flash Crash.* Retrieved from Bloomberg: https://www.bloomberg.com/opinion/articles/2015-04-21/guy-trading-at-home-caused-the-flash-crash

Levine, M. (2018, February 12). *Wells Fargo Sent People Free Money Too.* Retrieved from Bloomberg: https://www.bloomberg.com/opinion/articles/2018-02-12/wells-fargo-sent-people-free-money-too

Levine, M. (2019, November 5). *Playing the Game of Infinite Leverage.* Retrieved from Bloomberg: https://www.bloomberg.com/amp/opinion/articles/2019-11-05/playing-the-game-of-infinite-leverage

Lowenstein, R. (2010, April 19). *Gambling With the Economy.* Retrieved from New York Times: https://www.nytimes.com/2010/04/20/opinion/20lowenstein.html

Best of WSB

Ludwig, O. (2012, February 24). *Is UVXY Benefiting From TVIX's Woes?* Retrieved from ETF.com: https://www.etf.com/sections/features/11100-is-uvxy-benefiting-from-tvixs-woes.html

Maverick, J. (2018, June 18). *How Big Is the Derivatives Market?* Retrieved from Investopedia: https://www.investopedia.com/ask/answers/052715/how-big-derivatives-market.asp

MediaKix. (2019, December 13). *20 TIKTOK STATISTICS MARKETERS NEED TO KNOW: TIKTOK DEMOGRAPHICS & KEY DATA.* Retrieved from MediaKix: https://mediakix.com/blog/top-tik-tok-statistics-demographics/

Ordway, D.-M. (2019, August 6). *How journalists cover mass shootings: Research to consider.* Retrieved from Journalist's Resource: https://journalistsresource.org/studies/society/news-media/mass-shootings-news-research/

Pei, A. (2019, April 14). *This esports giant draws in more viewers than the Super Bowl, and it's expected to get even bigger.* Retrieved from CNBC: https://www.cnbc.com/2019/04/14/league-of-legends-gets-more-viewers-than-super-bowlwhats-coming-next.html

Popper, N. (2012, August 2). *Knight Capital Says Trading Glitch Cost It $440 Million.* Retrieved from New York Times: https://dealbook.nytimes.com/2012/08/02/knight-capital-says-trading-mishap-cost-it-440-million/

Post Flash Crash, Regulators Still Use Bicycles To Catch Ferraris. (2015, April 24). Retrieved from Traders Magazine: https://www.tradersmagazine.com/departments/technology/post-flash-crash-regulators-still-use-bicycles-to-catch-ferraris/

Pylypczak-Wasylyszyn, D. (2012, July 17). *46 Amusing ETF Ticker Symbols.* Retrieved from ETF Database: https://etfdb.com/2012/46-most-amusing-ticker-symbols/

Ramgopal, A. (2019, February 27). *Advisory Associate at PwC.* Retrieved from https://www.slideshare.net/: https://www.slideshare.net/AkhilRamgopal/robinhood-company-presentation-133614713

Robinson, M. (2019, 11 7). *Robinhood Is Back in Washington's Crosshairs After Leverage Glitch.* Retrieved from Bloomberg: https://www.bloomberg.com/amp/news/articles/2019-11-07/robinhood-back-in-washington-s-crosshairs-after-leverage-glitch

The Economist. (2019, October 7). *WOOF, CAKE, BOOM: stocks with catchy tickers beat the market.* Retrieved from The Economist: https://www.economist.com/graphic-detail/2019/10/07/woof-cake-boom-stocks-with-catchy-tickers-beat-the-market

Treanor, J. (2010, June 29). *Drunk trader banned for buying 7m barrels of oil after binge.* Retrieved from The Guardian: https://www.theguardian.com/business/2010/jun/29/drunk-oil-trader-banned-fsa

Turak, N. (2018, February 7). *Credit Suisse defends controversial financial product at the center of the market turmoil.* Retrieved from CNBC: https://www.cnbc.com/2018/02/07/credit-suisse-defends-controversial-xiv-etn-amid-market-turmoil.html

U.S. Congress. (2006, October 13). *Public Laws.* Retrieved from United States Publishing Printing Office: https://www.gpo.gov/fdsys/pkg/PLAW-109publ347/html/PLAW-109publ347.htm

Best of WSB

Wells Fargo. (2019, 06 01). *Millennials, Money, and the Happiness Factor.* Retrieved from Wells Fargo: https://www.wellsfargofunds.com/assets/edocs/marketing /sales-material/Millennials-money-happiness-factor-ss-nonlit-FASS389.pdf

Winck, B. (2019, December 2). *A Reddit trader claims to have found a new 'infinite money' glitch on Robinhood — but the company denies it exists.* Retrieved from Business Insider: https://markets.businessinsider.com/news/stocks/new-robinhood-infinite-leverage-free-glitch-found-reddit-trader-claims-2019-12-1028730335

World Federation of Exchanges database. (2019). *Market capitalization of listed domestic companies.* Retrieved from World Bank: https://data.worldbank.org/indicator/CM.MKT.LCAP.CD

Made in the USA
Monee, IL
23 February 2020